DELIGHTING IN THE KING OF KINGS

A Study on the Book of Matthew
Volume 2: Chapters 10–20

by Stacy Davis and Brenda Harris

 A Ministry of Calvary Chapel Chester Springs Women in Christ

Delighting in the King of Kings
A Study on the Book of Matthew
Volume 2: Chapters 10–20
Part of the Delighting in the Lord Bible Study Series

© Copyright 2019
Calvary Chapel Chester Springs
PO Box 595, Eagle, PA 19480

All rights reserved. No part of this book may be reproduced or transmitted in any form or by any means, electronic or mechanical, including photocopying and recording, or by any information storage or retrieval system, except as may be expressly permitted in writing by the publisher.

ISBN 9781081321000

Unless otherwise indicated, Scripture quotations are from the New King James Version of the Bible.
Copyright © 1982 by Thomas Nelson, Inc. Used by permission.
All rights reserved.

Ministry verse Psalm 27:4 is taken from the Holy Bible, New Living Translation (NLT),
copyright © 1996, 2004, 2015 by Tyndale House Foundation. Used by permission of Tyndale House Publishers, Inc., Carol Stream, Illinois 60188. All rights reserved.

Series Cover Design: Melissa Bereda
Cover Photo: Shutterstock

Printed in the United States of America

"The one thing I ask of the Lord - the thing I seek most - is to live in the house of the Lord all the days of my life, delighting in the Lord's perfections and meditating in his temple." Psalm 27:4

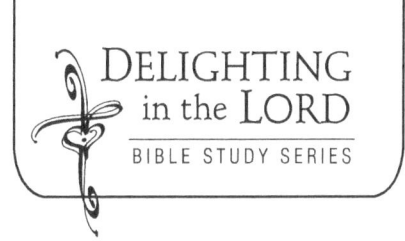

CONTENTS

DELIGHTING IN THE KING OF KINGS

A Study on the Book of Matthew
Volume 2: Chapters 10–20

Acknowledgments 6

About the Delighting in the Lord Ministry 7-8

Additional Studies 9

About the Authors 10

Introduction 11-12

R.E.A.D. Format 13

Delighting in My Salvation 14

Week 1   The King's Disciples:
         He Calls the Ordinary to Do the Extraordinary
         Matthew 10 15-30

Week 2   Misunderstood Expectations of the King
         Matthew 11 31-43

Week 3   The King Addresses His Critics
         Matthew 12 44-56

Week 4   The King Teaches in Parables About His Kingdom
         Matthew 13 57-71

Week 5   The King Provides for His People
         Matthew 14 72-84

Week 6   The King Lifts Burdens
         Matthew 15 85-97

CONTENTS

DELIGHTING IN THE KING OF KINGS

A Study on the Book of Matthew
Volume 2: Chapters 10–20

Week 7 The King Reinforces Spiritual Principles
        Matthew 16 98-113

Week 8 The King's Magnificence
        Matthew 17 114-124

Week 9 The King's Lessons on Humility
        Matthew 18 125-140

Week 10 The King Goes to the Heart
        Matthew 19 141-153

Week 11 Servant of the King
        Matthew 20 154-170

Bibliography 171

"Then Jesus said to His disciples,
'If anyone desires to come after Me,
let him deny himself,
and take up his cross,
and follow Me.'"
Matthew 16:24

"The one thing I ask of the Lord - the thing I seek most - is to live in the house of the Lord all the days of my life, delighting in the Lord's perfections and meditating in his temple." Psalm 27:4

ACKNOWLEDGMENTS

*"There are diversities of gifts, but the same Spirit.
There are differences of ministries, but the same Lord.
And there are diversities of activities but it is the same God who works all in all.
But the manifestation of the Spirit is given to each one for the profit of all."
1 Corinthians 12:4-7*

Many people with different gifts have come together for the common purpose of sharing God's Word (Matthew 28:19-20). This study is the product of those people and their gifts working together by God's grace. We are so thankful for each person and the role they fill.

Pastor Chris Swansen - Theological Editor, Calvary Chapel Chester Springs
Pastor Steven Dorr - Pastoral Support, Calvary Chapel Chester Springs
Carinna LaRocco - Copy Editor
Joan Purdy - Copy Editor
Melissa Bereda - Graphic Designer
Lynn Jensen - Office Support
Chris Good - Photographer

A huge thank you as well to the families that allow us to use their second homes for writing getaways.

Additionally, we could not fulfill this calling without the love and support of our husbands and children. From the time God called us to write women's Bible studies, we have considered the call "our reasonable act of service" (Romans 12:1) to Him. Our families and those involved in the DITL ministry join us in this calling. We pray these studies will be used by God to draw many deeper into His Word to the heart of God so that lives and relationships will be transformed by His great power and grace.

With love in Christ,
Stacy and Brenda
Delighting in the Lord Ministry

"The one thing I ask of the Lord - the thing I seek most - is to live in the house of the Lord all the days of my life, delighting in the Lord's perfections and meditating in his temple." Psalm 27:4

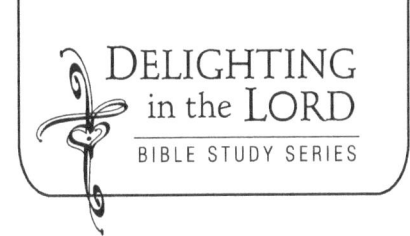

ABOUT THE DELIGHTING IN THE LORD MINISTRY

In 2006, Stacy and Brenda were separately called by the Lord to begin ministering to women. Stacy began teaching a Thursday morning Bible study for women at her home church, Calvary Chapel Chester Springs. Each Thursday the ladies met for Bible teaching and small group discussion. Meanwhile, Brenda began a traveling teaching ministry called Life Applications Ministries. Their paths would not cross for two more years. What they did not know was God would form a partnership to fulfill both of their callings, together, in a way neither of them would have foreseen. God was laying the groundwork for the Delighting in the Lord Ministry.

In 2008, Stacy asked Brenda to join the Thursday Bible study as a small group leader. The small group leaders helped with the teaching load, and this became the first year that Stacy and Brenda ministered together.

For the next two years, Brenda and Stacy taught the women who gathered on Thursday mornings using Bible study materials from other Calvary Chapel churches and authors. In 2010, Stacy was diagnosed with invasive breast cancer, and Brenda became more hands-on in the women's ministry. It was during that year that God planted the writing seeds in Stacy and Brenda's hearts. Sensing the Lord's direction to study the book of Matthew the following year, Brenda and Stacy searched for a women's Bible study on Matthew. They found nothing that covered the whole book in a verse-by-verse format with an emphasis on life applications. As Stacy prayed seeking God's direction, God continued speaking to her heart, telling her to "write the study." With much fear and trepidation, Stacy shared this with Brenda who also began diligently praying for God's direction. As Brenda sought the Lord, He gave her the READ format vision, and then He gave them both Psalm 27:4 which became their ministry verse and foundation:

"The one thing I ask of the Lord, the thing I seek most, is to live in the house of the Lord all my life, delighting in the Lord's perfections, and meditating in His temple." (NLT)

After much prayer and with the faith to believe that since God called them He would equip them, the Delighting in the Lord Bible Study Series was birthed that year.

2011 was spent studying and writing "Delighting in the King," a women's Bible study on the book of Matthew. God brought many key people to support the work including Pastor Chris Swansen, who read every page of the study for Biblical accuracy. Seeing the need, God also touched the hearts of two women, Carinna LaRocco and Joan Purdy, who became our copy editors. They review our written words and make sure our studies are without writing errors. He also provided a graphic designer, Melissa Bereda. She has designed all of the logos, covers, and interior pages. Each person God brought to partner with Stacy and Brenda in this ministry has answered God's call on their life to use their gifts for God's glory.

The next year, upon suggestion from the ladies attending the Thursday morning study, the teaching sessions were video recorded and the church began putting all the materials online. These teaching videos are available at www.delightinginthelord.com. Since then, God has used Brenda and Stacy to teach His Word, both in written and spoken form, to the women who gather together on Thursday mornings as well as to women online, individuals, and those in other study groups and churches.

What began as a simple "Yes, God" became a ministry that teaches God's Word to women, drawing out His truths and life applications. They are simply two women who love Jesus with their whole hearts and lives. They have experienced the power of the cross in their own lives and want to tell others of the saving power and grace of Jesus, so others can live a life of peace and joy in the midst of life's chaos. Even more, so that others can live with hope, knowing their eternal home with Jesus awaits. They are humbled hearing testimonies of God's transforming work of the Holy Spirit as women have used these studies to delve into God's Word.

"The one thing I ask of the Lord - the thing I seek most - is to live in the house of the Lord all the days of my life, delighting in the Lord's perfections and meditating in his temple." Psalm 27:4

ADDITIONAL STUDIES IN THE DELIGHTING IN THE LORD BIBLE STUDY SERIES

Each verse-by-verse study is inductive and deductive with life application emphasis following the **READ** format: **Receiving** God's word, **Experiencing** God's word, **Acting** on God's word, and **Delighting** in God's word.

Delighting in God, His Righteousness and Perfect Plan: Romans

Delighting in Being a Child of God: 1, 2 & 3 John

Delighting in God's Will and His Provision: Jonah & Nahum

Delighting in the Redeemer, a Love Story: Ruth

Delighting in God's Heart: A study on the Life of David through 1 & 2 Samuel and the Psalms

Delighting in The Holy Spirit: Acts

Delighting in Being a Woman of God: Esther

Delighting in a Life Lived for God: 1 Peter (Amazon 2020)

Delighting in A Life of Triumph: A study on the life of Joseph from Genesis 37–50 (Amazon)

Delighting in God's Wisdom: Proverbs (Amazon)

Delighting in the King of Kings: Matthew Volume 1: Chapters 1–9 (Amazon)

For additional information about the ministry, please go to:
www.delightinginthelord.com.
All studies and videos of corresponding teachings are available at:
www.cc-chestersprings.com/DITL.
A few of the studies are available for purchase on Amazon.com (see above).

"The one thing I ask of the Lord - the thing I seek most - is to live in the house of the Lord all the days of my life, delighting in the Lord's perfections and meditating in his temple." Psalm 27:4

ABOUT THE AUTHORS

STACY DAVIS has been teaching women God's Word for over 15 years. She has learned many Biblical truths through difficult trials. Beginning at the age of three with her mother's brain aneurism, to the death of her fourth son and through invasive breast cancer, Stacy's faith has been tried and tested many times over. Her life gives testimony to God's redeeming and transforming power. Stacy teaches with passion the truths of God's Word, desiring to share with all women how to go through everyday struggles victoriously in Jesus Christ. She lives in PA with her husband, Barclay. They have six children.

BRENDA HARRIS's background in education, along with her many years as a classroom teacher, were foundational for the plans God had for her to serve Him. In 2006, she transitioned away from instructing young people how to read literature and began teaching women they can have a closer walk with the Lord through reading and studying their Bible. She is an enthusiastic teacher who loves a great visual to help demonstrate practical ways to apply God's Word to real life. Brenda lives in PA with her husband, Michael, and their two children.

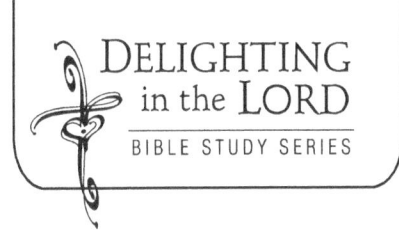

"The one thing I ask of the Lord - the thing I seek most - is to live in the house of the Lord all the days of my life, delighting in the Lord's perfections and meditating in his temple." Psalm 27:4

INTRODUCTION
DELIGHTING IN THE KING OF KINGS

A Study on the Book of Matthew
Volume 2: Chapters 10–20

The book of Matthew will forever remain dear to Stacy and me (Brenda). In 2011 God called us to write a Bible study on the book of Matthew, and in answer to God's call, we wrote our very first Bible study, Delighting in the King: A Study on the Book of Matthew. We were brand new Bible study authors at the time, and often the study pages were completed just weeks prior to putting them into the hands of the women attending the Thursday morning study at Calvary Chapel Chester Springs in PA. It was a giant undertaking. Now we can look back in amazement at how God equipped us to do the work He was calling us to do. We truly had no idea the journey we were embarking upon! Eight years later and many other studies written, we felt the Lord call us to revise our first study on the book of Matthew. It is with great joy we share this updated version with you.

"The Gospel According to Matthew" is the first of the four gospels in the New Testament. It was written by a Jewish tax collector named Matthew who was one of Jesus' disciples. He wrote his account about Jesus' life and works in the hope other Jews would recognize their Messiah had come. Jesus had fulfilled all the prophecies that were recorded for them in the Old Testament. Curiously, you will not find one spoken word by Matthew recorded in any of the four Gospels; yet, his written words in the book of Matthew speak loud and clear. His objective was not to be known himself but to point others to The One more important than him, Jesus Christ, the Messiah.

This study is broken apart into three volumes. This volume includes chapters 10–20 which covers Jesus' teachings, miracles, and difficult interactions with the Jewish leadership. The contents of these eleven chapters are full of amazing eyewitness accounts of what Jesus did while He lived among mankind. Jesus' disciples were full of hope because their long-awaited Messiah had finally come to earth. They witnessed Jesus heal, feed, and teach the multitudes of people. Doing this proved to His followers that He was the Messiah. Many believed, but some didn't.

Jesus' popularity was growing daily, and many thought He would free them from living under the harsh Roman rule and set up the prophesied kingdom. However, Jesus frequently reminded the disciples that before His kingdom could be established, there would have to be suffering, pain, and death. First comes suffering, then comes glory. This truth was perplexing and hard for them to understand, and yet Jesus patiently foretold the future to them. While the multitudes and disciples grew to love Jesus more and more each day, the Jewish leadership's hatred for Jesus grew. This hatred would blossom into a full-blown plan to kill Jesus which will unfold in volume three of our study.

Whether you are a first-time Bible study participant, or you have been studying the Bible for years, the book of Matthew inspires new learning for all of us. Take the time to sit and read the words recorded about the unparalleled life of Jesus Christ. Think about how His life changed not only the lives of the Jewish readers over 2,000 years ago but also your life today as a woman seeking to know her Savior better. From the first cries of the baby Jesus to the cry He will call out from upon the cross, Jesus came for all of us. He came to save mankind from their suffering and their sins. There is none like Him, Jesus Christ, the King of Kings.

AUTHOR
Matthew, also known as Levi, the son of Alpheus, was Jewish. He was a tax collector who belonged to the class of people most bitterly hated by the Jews. A tax collector was considered a Roman employee and seen as working for the enemy of Jerusalem. No Jew wanted to be associated with a tax collector, but God chose Matthew to not only be one of His disciples but also to be a Gospel writer. Additionally, as a tax collector, a portion of Matthew's life was spent managing money. It is not surprising that as he pens the book, he references coins several times (Matthew 17:24, 27 and Matthew 18:24). Yet, interestingly, he omits two parables about tax collectors which the Gospel of Luke includes (Luke 18, 19).

PURPOSE
As the first book in the New Testament, Matthew links the Old Testament with the New Testament. Matthew's primary goal is to prove how Jesus fulfills the Old Testament prophecies and is the Jews' long-awaited Messiah.

DATE
Approximately 50 A.D. (as early as 37 A.D. but most likely before 70 A.D.)

WEEKLY WRITTEN LESSONS
This three-volume study on Matthew is a verse-by-verse expository approach to studying the Bible. The first volume contains chapters 1–9, the second volume examines chapters 10–20, and the third covers chapters 21–28.

Each week you will only go through the R.E.A.D. format once in your homework. You may choose to do the homework in one sitting or in many; it is totally up to you. You should plan on about 60-90 minutes to complete the whole week's study. We highly encourage you to spend the time in God's Word answering these questions and digging into the text for yourself. You will find that your time investment will be given back to you deeply for your spiritual growth.

When you see this scroll symbol next to a question, it is an indicator that the question includes prophecy about the Messiah and how Jesus fulfilled that prophecy. Since this was one of the primary reasons Matthew wrote this Gospel, we felt it was important for these questions to stand out from the rest with a special marking.

"The one thing I ask of the Lord - the thing I seek most - is to live in the house of the Lord all the days of my life, delighting in the Lord's perfections and meditating in his temple." Psalm 27:4

FORMAT: "READ" THE BIBLE

*The format for this study follows the acronym **READ**: Read the Bible.*

RECEIVING God's Word

1. **Open in Prayer:** Before reading God's word, you need to prepare your heart to receive from Him what He has for you.
- During this time of prayer, confess any sin that may be present in your life.
- Ask God to open "the eyes of your heart" (Eph 1:18) so you can hear from Him what He wants to communicate to you.
- Thank Him in advance for what He will do!
2. **Receiving**: Read the scripture text given.

EXPERIENCING God's Word

This is where you will dive into the Bible and the daily chapter/verses. You'll be answering questions that lead you through the text by first observing the details and then focusing on the connections within the text to the bigger picture. At other times, you may be investigating other verses from the whole counsel of God and then drawing some Biblical conclusions from what you have read. There may be several "experiences" drawn from the text.

ACTING on God's Word

In this part of the study you will be applying these verses to your life. We read in Hebrews 4:12 that God's word is "living and powerful, and sharper than any two-edged sword, piercing even to the division of soul and spirit, and of joints and marrow, and is a discerner of the thoughts and intents of the heart." Therefore, as you are studying, God will be speaking to your heart and life. We will be encouraging you to look at applications, but God may have other things He is speaking to your heart. We pray you hear directly from Him. As you listen to the Lord speak to your heart, may He show you what steps He desires you take as you walk out your faith in Him.

DELIGHTING in God's Word

In this final section you will reflect upon what you have learned and offer up your praise and thanksgiving to the Lord. As you close out your daily time, may you truly find that He is the delight of your heart! He fills like no other and nothing else can. And as you "delight yourself in the LORD" He will give you the desires of your heart (Psalm 37:4); because after studying His word, your desires and His should be the same. Through your time in God's word, may you grow more and more into His image. You will be asked to record a verse (or as many as you want!) that stood out to you from the text and then memorize it if you so desire.

"The one thing I ask of the Lord - the thing I seek most - is to live in the house of the Lord all the days of my life, delighting in the Lord's perfections and meditating in his temple." Psalm 27:4

DELIGHTING IN MY SALVATION

If you have never accepted Jesus Christ as your Savior but desire to take that step of faith, all you need to do is:

Recognize that God loves you!
"For God so loved the world that He gave His only begotten Son, that whoever believes in Him should not perish but have everlasting life." (John 3:16)

"But God demonstrates His own love toward us, in that while we were still sinners, Christ died for us." (Romans 5:8)

Admit you are a sinner.
For all have sinned and fall short of the glory of God." (Romans 3:23)

"As it is written: 'There is none righteous, no, not one;' " (Romans 3:10)

Recognize Jesus Christ as being God's only remedy for sin.
"For the wages of sin is death, but the gift of God is eternal life in Christ Jesus our Lord." (Romans 6:23)

"But as many as received Him, to them He gave the right to become children of God, to those who believe in His name:" (John 1:12)

"For I delivered to you first of all that which I also received: that Christ died for our sins according to the Scriptures, and that He was buried, and that He rose again the third day according to the Scriptures." (1 Corinthians 15:3-4)

Receive Jesus Christ as your personal Savior!
"If you confess with your mouth the Lord Jesus and believe in your heart that God has raised Him from the dead, you will be saved." (Romans 10:9)

Prayer is simply "talking with God." Right now, go to God in prayer and ask Christ to be your Savior. You might pray something like this:

"Lord Jesus, I need You. I confess that I am a sinner and that You paid the penalty for my sin through Your death on the cross. I believe that You died for my sins and were raised from the dead. I ask You to come into my heart, take control of my life, and make me the kind of person that You want me to be. Thank You for coming into my life as You promised." Amen.

If you have prayed to accept Christ as your Savior, please tell someone today! Share this exciting news with a close Christian friend, your small group leader or your pastor. They will be thrilled to encourage you in your faith and your decision to follow Jesus!

"The one thing I ask of the Lord - the thing I seek most - is to live in the house of the Lord all the days of my life, delighting in the Lord's perfections and meditating in his temple." Psalm 27:4

WEEK 1

THE KING'S DISCIPLES: HE CALLS THE ORDINARY TO DO THE EXTRAORDINARY

Matthew 10

Matthew 4:23 tells us Jesus traveled through Galilee, taught in the synagogues, preached the Gospel of the kingdom, and healed all kinds of sickness and disease. Over and over again, Jesus demonstrated His heavenly kingship, His authority over the powers of darkness, and His healing power in the lives of mankind. Jews and Gentiles alike were drawn to Jesus. They followed Him in droves—going where He went, sitting at His feet, and leaning in to hear all He had to say. Many came needing His power and authority in their lives.

Chapter 9 ends with Matthew telling us that Jesus was moved with compassion for the people. Countless times He saw their need; the pain in their eyes, the emptiness in their hearts, and their weary faces. Moved with compassion, Jesus met them in their need, wanting them to know that His Kingdom was for them. He was their Savior and wanted to be their King. The world needed to know Him. There were so many hurting and trapped in sin. But who would be His mouthpiece? Who would represent Him to the people outside Jerusalem?

He chose twelve—Twelve ordinary men who Jesus would empower to do extraordinary things in His name.

In chapter 10 we hear Jesus' ordination sermon given to the twelve disciples to encourage and prepare them for the mission that lay ahead. These twelve were called personally by Jesus and were given His power. The Master bestowed on the student what was His. These men were to be His mouthpiece, His hands and feet, and His Kingdom representatives to the hurting Jews throughout Galilee. From a tax collector to fishermen and tradesmen, these men didn't have credentials or long resumes detailing their readiness for the job at hand. But that's exactly what Jesus wanted. What they lacked in physical abilities, Jesus made up for through spiritual power. He worked in hearts surrendered to Him. What they said and did would come from Jesus' anointing and empowerment.

Jesus' call to each of us can easily get mixed with our own uncertainty and feeling of inadequacy. I (Stacy) know that to be true of the call God has placed on my life.

Never in my wildest imagination did I think I would ever be a Bible teacher and Bible study writer. Never! In college I studied communications and writing but had way different plans for its practical use. I remember the day God called me to first teach His Word, and then I began writing women's Bible studies a few years later. The cry of my heart initially was, "I can't, Lord! I'm not a Bible scholar. I didn't attend Bible college. I love You and your Word, but what You are asking is beyond me." That is often right where He wants us! Every time I said, "I can't," Jesus reassured me that I could in His power and authority. He prepared me, called me, and equipped me to be His mouthpiece to women. In my own unworthiness and deficiency, I have found His grace and power more than sufficient even in the midst of critical voices, obstacles, and many trials.

Each one of us has been created by God for His special purposes. He has gifted you. He will empower you for wherever and whatever He calls you to. God chooses ordinary men and women to carry out His will here on earth, pointing the lost and hurting to Jesus. He does the extraordinary through those who seek to serve Him. Are you willing? Will you go where He sends you? Let's look at what He has to say to the twelve disciples as they get ready to go to the lost sheep of Israel and see what He wants to teach us.

RECEIVING God's Word

Open in Prayer
Read Matthew 10

EXPERIENCING God's Word

Experience 1: Read Matthew 10:1–15

1. Read Matthew 10:1. Jesus gives an invitation to twelve ordinary men. He calls these men to Himself and gives them power to do extraordinary things. List what they are now equipped to do.

2. Read Matthew 10:1–2. In verse 1 Matthew refers to the twelve men as disciples. In verse 2 they are now called apostles. A disciple means "a student or learner." An apostle means "a messenger or a delegate sent forth with orders." Why is it important to have both qualifications as a representative of Jesus?

3. Matthew lists the names of Jesus' twelve disciples in verses 2–4. Who are they? Write anything you know about each of them.

4. Look at Matthew 10:5–6. Jesus gives two commands to His disciples. What are these commands?

a. Read Romans 1:16. What do you learn that supports the commission given to the disciples in these verses?

b. Read Acts 3:24–26. Who needed to first accept Jesus as King? (This goes along with the promise God gave to Abraham in Genesis 12:3.)

c. The Jews looked forward for centuries to the coming of the King Messiah and the unveiling of His dominion over all the earth. They were the chosen people. But Jesus came to save us all from our sins. Read Acts 13:46–48. What did many of the Jews do with the King and His message? How did this open the door for the Gentiles?

5. Jesus gave His disciples further instructions in Matthew 10:7–8. From what you learned in verse 1, list their additional responsibilities. Part of the new instructions included their message. According to verses 7–8, what was the message they were to share, and why was this a necessary starting point of their message?

6. In Matthew 10:8 Jesus reminded His disciples what they received from Him was given freely. Why might Jesus have given them this reminder as He sent them out as His messengers?

7. Read Matthew 10:9–13. Jesus now addresses their conduct as they travel. Describe how the disciples were to travel and where they were to stay along the way.

a. We see the word *worthy* four times in verses 10–13. Use verses 11–13a to compare and contrast what the disciples were to give a worthy and unworthy household.

b. Why do you think it was important for them to stay with those who were worthy?

c. We read in verse 15 that judgment was to be brought against those who were not hospitable or worthy to receive the disciples. In Genesis 19 Sodom and Gomorrah were destroyed because of their lack of righteousness. With this in mind, why would Jesus have given the command in verse 14 to His disciples?

Experience 2: Read Matthew 10:16–26

1. In verse 16 Jesus uses imagery. He describes how the disciples are to behave and compares them to four animals. Compare and contrast each animal's attribute and the actions Jesus wants the disciples to demonstrate.

    Sheep –

    Wolves –

    Serpents –

    Doves –

2. Jesus cautions His disciples in verses 17–23. In His warning He says three groups will come against the disciples. List the three groups as seen in verses 17, 18, and 21. In verses 19 and 22–23 Jesus gives them some encouragement in the face of persecution. Describe His encouragement.

    a. Read 2 Corinthians 4:16–18. How do these verses bring a deeper understanding of Matthew 10:16–23?

3. In Matthew 10:22b Jesus tells His disciples, "But he who endures to the end will be saved." Jesus will later say the same thing in Matthew 24:13–14. Read the verses in Matthew 24. Was Jesus speaking of literal salvation through faithful devotion? Explain your answer. What end was He speaking of?

4. Read Matthew 10:24–26. The powers Jesus gave his disciples mimicked His own. Think about the powers found in Matthew 10:1 & 8. How do these powers liken the disciples to Jesus and prove His authority?

Delighting in the King of Kings

   a. In verses 25–26 Jesus tells the disciples that He has been accused of being called a servant of Beelzebub (the devil) as He demonstrated His powers. As the Master speaks from experience, what encouragement does He give His servants?

Experience 3: Read Matthew 10:27–42

1. Read Matthew 10:27. What are we to publicly profess, or confess, despite what may result?

2. Read Matthew 10:28–31. Jesus uses the illustration of a sparrow as He speaks to the disciples. What does He say about God's love for the sparrow?

   a. How should this demonstrate God's love for the disciples despite difficult circumstances?

b. How should this analogy be used to help them overcome their fear?

3. According to verses 32–33, what should every believer be doing? What eternal consequences are there for not obeying these commands?

4. Read Matthew 10:34–36. The Jews were looking for the Messiah to come, to set up His kingdom, and to bring peace to the nation. Jesus tells them in verse 34 that He did not come to bring peace on earth; instead, He brought a sword. Describe the purpose of the division being brought by the sword.

5. Read Matthew 10:37–39. Jesus speaks to the disciples' affections. He makes three comparisons. These are listed below. He also used the word *worthy* three more times in talking about affections and discipleship. Think about the comparison being used and describe the essence of these affections.

Affections	Description of Affection
Father/Mother (v. 37)	
Son/Daughter (v. 37)	
Willingness to take up cross (instrument used for death of self) (v. 38)	

a. In Matthew 10:39 Jesus says, "He who finds his life will lose it, and he who loses his life for My sake will find it." How might these affections interfere with being a disciple?

6. According to verses 40–42, what is in store for all who receive Christ's messengers and aid them in their witness?

   a. Read 1 Corinthians 3:9–17. Describe how God's disciples will be rewarded for the work they accomplished while living on earth.

7. Write a short description of Jesus as the King of Kings from what you learned in this chapter.

 **ACTING on God's Word**

"And Jesus said to Simon, 'Do not be afraid. From now on you will catch men.' So, when they had brought their boats to land, they forsook all and followed Him." These words from Luke 5:10b–11 were the verses God used to call me (Brenda) into ministry. I vividly remember reading this passage many years ago when God quietly called me to put aside my own pursuits to follow His directions for my life. I felt ill-equipped and unworthy, with

no idea how I would begin ministering for Him, but I willingly agreed in my heart to step out in faith. Since then, God has faithfully equipped me, taught me, helped me overcome obstacles, and continues to send me forth in His power to do what He calls me to do for Him.

In our text we meet the twelve men Jesus called to represent Him. They each forsook their life's agenda and picked up God's. For some, this is not an easy decision, but for those who choose it, they find it comes with rewards that outweigh anything they could gain in this life. Let's take a look at how God calls and equips as well as the instruction He gives regarding conduct and obstacles before sending a disciple forth to represent Him.

1. <u>The Calling</u>
   Based on what you learned from the text in Matthew 10, what might it look like in our culture today for God to "call" someone into ministry?

   a. Ministry can take many forms as it did in Matthew 10:2. What are some of the ways God might ask you to minister for Him?

2. <u>The Equipping</u>
   Jesus equipped His apostles, who were just ordinary men, to do extraordinary things because of the power He gave them in Matthew 10:1. How does God give us similar power today to minister in His name?

   a. List several ways you can cooperate with the Holy Spirit that allows Him to demonstrate His power through your life.

3. <u>Conduct</u>
   Jesus gave specific instructions on how a disciple should behave. Why do you think that is important?

    a. If you call yourself a Christian, then you want to be worthy of representing Jesus well. How does your daily conduct reflect being a sheep among wolves? Is your behavior wise as a serpent but gentle as a dove?

4. <u>Obstacles</u>
Jesus warned His disciples there would be obstacles put in their way to make their jobs difficult. He told them to look out for conflict in relationships, with the government, with religious authorities, and even from the satanic realm. In what ways have you encountered similar challenges when involved in ministry for Christ?

5. <u>Sending Forth</u>
It is mentioned in Mark 6:7 that Jesus sent out the twelve men in pairs. Matthew does not include this detail; however, it is something interesting to consider. Why would it be helpful to have a ministry partner?

DELIGHTING in God's Word

From Matthew 10, how has the Lord prompted you to pray?

Write a verse from the chapter that God has spoken to your heart.

Close in Prayer

"The one thing I ask of the Lord - the thing I seek most - is to live in the house of the Lord all the days of my life, delighting in the Lord's perfections and meditating in his temple." Psalm 27:4

WEEK 2
MISUNDERSTOOD EXPECTATIONS OF THE KING
Matthew 11

His body was still and lifeless. He had passed away when I (Brenda) was not there. I leaned down to hug my dad one last time, and my tears soaked his chest. As I stood and considered my new horrible reality, disappointment with God flooded my soul. The demanding questions shouted at God in my head, "Where are You? Why did You allow this to happen? I know You are more than capable of healing him, yet You have not!" The weight of my unmet expectations with God began to crush me, and anger rose up inside of me. Those would be some of the last words I would spew at God for an entire year. I checked out and grew very bitter.

Yet, He did not leave me there. With His everlasting kindness and love, God drew me back to Himself. When I returned to Him, He graciously showed me where I went wrong. Instead of trusting and accepting what God deemed best for my dad's life, I had demanded my desires to be fulfilled. I expected God to heal Dad and to spare me from experiencing the sting of death for as long as possible. I wanted God to meet my expectations and to fulfill my plan, in my timing. I wish I could say I am unique, but sadly, Matthew 11 reminds me I am not.

The Jews, including John the Baptist, had expectations for what they believed the Messiah would do when He came to earth. He should fulfill the prophecies the way they anticipated. He should do it in their timing and their way. He should rule and reign immediately and usher in peace and prosperity for the Jews. And yet, these events did not happen the way they expected, and therefore, some became bitter and angry.

As I consider what is written in Matthew 11, I recognize I was not much different from the Jews in Jesus' day. I, like the generation described in Matthew 11:17, said of God, "We played the flute for you, and you did not dance, we mourned to you, and you did not lament." They wanted God to perform for them like a playmate and so did I. This type of expectation not only is sin but boxes God into a place where He does not belong. When we trust God to be God and not our marionette, we will find rest for our souls (Matthew 11:29) and experience His best for our life.

R RECEIVING God's Word

Open in Prayer
Read Matthew 11

E EXPERIENCING God's Word

Matthew 11:1–30

1. Read Matthew 11:1–3. John the Baptist is in prison. In Matthew 14:3–5 we learn that John rebuked King Herod for an immoral relationship with his half-sister, Herodias. As a result, Herod wanted to kill John but did not because the people considered him a prophet. While John is in prison, word gets back to him about Jesus' works. How does John respond?

    a. Read John 1:29–34. What did the Holy Spirit reveal to John the Baptist?

b. Read Matthew 3:7–12. What was John's expectations of the Messiah?

c. With your answers to questions a and b in mind, why did John question Jesus as the Messiah?

2. How does Jesus respond to John's question in Matthew 11:4–6?

a. Read Isaiah 61:1. This verse should have been common knowledge to John the Baptist and the Jews. How does this verse confirm Jesus as the Messiah?

3. Read Matthew 11:7–11. In your own words, how did Jesus describe John the Baptist?

   a. Read Malachi 3:1. How did Jesus' description in Matthew 11:10 authenticate both John's ministry and His own?

> "Though John was great, he was not born again under the New Covenant. This is because he lived and died before the completion of Jesus' work at the cross and empty tomb. Therefore, he did not enjoy the benefits of the New Covenant (1 Corinthians 11:25, 2 Corinthians 3:6, Hebrews 8:6–13)." (David Guzik, EnduringWord.com)

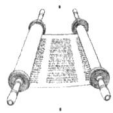

4. Read Matthew 11:12–15. In verse 12 Jesus is saying that hostility has arisen since the days of John the Baptist until the time He is speaking in this verse. Who has been forceful against John, and who will eventually be forceful against Jesus?

a. What effect does this have on the establishment of God's kingdom?

5. Read Matthew 11:13–14. We are told that the Prophets and Law prophesied of Jesus' coming. Verse 14 tells us that John is Elijah who is to come, but Jesus gives a condition. What is the condition? How did the Jews receive John?

   a. Read Luke 1:17. How does this verse further describe John and his purpose?

   b. Read Malachi 3:1 again. This prophesy refers to the first coming of Christ. Now read Malachi 4:4–5. This prophecy refers to the second coming of Christ. The Jews did not understand the scope of this prophecy as well as the impact their rejection would have on this prophecy, and so they misinterpret it regarding John the Baptist. Who will come before the Lord establishes His kingdom, and why did this create confusion?

    c. Read John 1:19–23. How does John answer the Pharisees' question about his identity? As he stated his purpose, he quoted Isaiah 40:3. Why were the Pharisees confused about John's identity and purpose based on prophecy?

    d. Read Matthew 17:10–13. What does Jesus say to His disciples about Elijah and John the Baptist?

6. In Matthew 11:15 Jesus exhorts His listeners to have ears to hear. Summarize why His words are hard for them to understand.

7. In verses 16–19 Jesus is pointing out that the current generation has unmet expectations. Explain how verses 16–19 support this. List how the Jews felt about Jesus up until this point and how John the Baptist did not fulfill their expectations.

a. Jesus ends verse 19 by saying, "But wisdom [Jesus] is justified by her children." Explain the point Jesus is trying to make.

8. Read Matthew 11:20–24 and answer the following questions:

a. Jesus rebukes cities for their lack of repentance despite His display of power in those cities. It is not recorded what Jesus did in these cities, yet the judgment He will pass on them is warranted by His rebuke. Describe the rebuke to Chorazin and Bethsaida. Who does He compare them to?

b. Why does Jesus' presence and works in those cities hold them to a higher level of accountability?

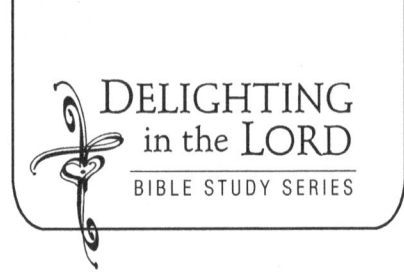

    c. What is Jesus' rebuke to Capernaum? Who does He compare Capernaum to?

    d. From these verses, it is clear that God has varying levels of judgment for those who are more exposed to the truth of Jesus Christ. How was this a grave warning?

> "Chorazin, Bethsaida, and Capernaum were all destroyed in the 6th century by an earthquake estimated to be 7.8 on the Richter Scale." (Ido Keynan, Israeli Archeologist)

9. Read Matthew 11:25. Jesus begins speaking to the Father, the Lord of heaven and earth. Describe the gratefulness Jesus expresses to God regarding what He just taught on.

10. Read Matthew 11:26–27. How does Jesus describe the authority and power of God?

11. Jesus is calling the people to Himself in verses 28–30. What does He see in the people that makes Him extend this invitation?

   a. What does Jesus offer to remedy their condition?

   b. Describe why rejection creates unrest.

12. Write a short description of Jesus as the King of Kings from what you learned in this chapter.

A ACTING on God's Word

We've all had them: Unmet, selfish, misunderstood and wrongfully placed expectations. Expectations have a way of creating unrest, disappointment, and even worse, division among people. We saw this very thing in Matthew 11 as John the Baptist had unmet expectations of the Messiah. He didn't understand God's timing,

yet he called Him the Lamb of God. He anticipated the Messiah to bring judgment to the rebellious people and to establish His kingdom. He knew what the Messiah would do for the people when He came but didn't understand the timetable or the consequences of the Jew's rejection. Doubt crept into John the Baptist's mind that he seemed to act on from prison.

The Jews also had unmet expectations mixed with perceived hopes regarding John the Baptist and Jesus. These expectations were encased in pride, causing the Jews to reject Jesus. They anticipated the Messiah would make their lives peaceful and elevate their status. Their expectations were self-serving, as expectations often are. Because of this, their rejection of Jesus and lack of repentance would have consequences not only for themselves but also for the nation of Israel.

I (Stacy) can fall victim to expectations too. One of my favorite verses to remember when I see myself placing expectations on others is Psalm 62:5–6a. "My soul waits silently for God alone, for my expectation is from Him. He only is my rock and my salvation." In Him alone—I will never be disappointed when I surrender to His authority, trusting Him to act according to His will and not mine. People will often disappoint and fail me especially when I expect them to act according to my plan or needs. But I am reminded that when my expectation is in God, my soul is at rest.

Let's apply what we learned in Matthew 11 about expectations.

1. Can you think of a time when you set expectations on God for something that was not about Him and His character but rather about your will and desire for Him to act a certain way on your behalf? Describe this time. What have you learned that you can apply to this situation?

2. Describe how humility impacts expectations.

3. For the believer, God sets our expectations in Scripture in certain areas of life. For example, God says that children are to obey their parents in Colossians 3:20. God says in Ephesians 5:25 that husbands are to love their wives as Christ loves the church and gave Himself for her. These are God-given expectations we can have. Yet, often people let us down and do not follow God's expectations. How do you respond when this happens? How should you respond? Explain why your response to unmet expectations matters to God.

4. In Matthew 11 Jesus likened the Jewish population at the time to children. Their behavior was childish. From what Jesus said in Matthew 11:17, the Jews wanted to be the puppet master and Jesus the puppet. Have you ever fallen into this trap of trying to manipulate people to act according to your expectations only to see them not cooperate? Who do you place the greater expectations upon? Describe how this is childish behavior.

5. Jesus ended Matthew 11 by offering rest to His people. He saw His people struggling and not entering into the refreshment and contentment that He alone provides for them. How do expectations often cause unrest? How do expectations become burdensome and laborious?

 **D** **DELIGHTING** in God's Word

From Matthew 11, how has the Lord prompted you to pray?

Write a verse from the chapter that God has spoken to your heart.

Close in Prayer

"The one thing I ask of the Lord - the thing I seek most - is to live in the house of the Lord all the days of my life, delighting in the Lord's perfections and meditating in his temple." Psalm 27:4

WEEK 3
THE KING ADDRESSES HIS CRITICS
Matthew 12

It had become apparent that she was upset with me (Stacy). Her interactions with me had grown tense, and her words were curt, lacking respect that once permeated our relationship. I knew when she reached out to me for a meeting that words would be exchanged; I just wasn't prepared for the depth of the criticism that awaited me that day. We sat across from each other and accusations poured out of her as she tore me down as a women's ministry leader. I listened quietly at first, letting her say her peace. Her words stung and dug deep into my heart. She was criticizing me in ways that were unexpected and harsh. And then she turned the conversation to my walk with Jesus. Her claims elevated her relationship to Jesus while questioning mine. It was all I could do to sit still and receive what she said. With the little defenses I offered, she just got more frustrated. Eventually, she stood up and ended our meeting by abruptly walking out of the room. I sat there in disbelief as to what just happened and the words that were spoken about me. Tears streamed down my face as I processed through her criticism and the shattered pieces of our relationship that clearly resulted.

The dictionary defines criticism as the "expression of disapproval of someone or something on the basis of perceived faults or mistakes, the analysis and judgment of said things." Note that criticism often comes from the place of perception. Often, we criticize that which we don't understand or makes us feel lesser. We first compare, then criticize in that comparison. Criticism always elevates self and devalues another. Pride is its root, and anger is its result.

In Matthew 12 Jesus comes under the methodical and calculated criticism of the Pharisees and religious leaders of the time. Their intent seems to be self-serving in an effort to elevate themselves in religious superiority while trying to damage Jesus' witness and testimony. From grain fields, to the synagogue, and to the streets, the Pharisees try to tear down Jesus. Their accusations come through His healings and expressions of compassion. As Jesus extends grace and love to the hungry, the disabled, and the demon-possessed, the religious leaders accuse Jesus of breaking Jewish law and being influenced by satanic powers. They demand a sign from Jesus so He could prove His deity and authority. Jesus is swift to bring truth to their perceived faults of Him. Even more, Jesus takes their criticism and turns it back on them. He measures them with the same standard they were measuring Him. Jesus tears down their accusations while providing no defense other than truth from God.

Delighting in the King of Kings

There is much we can learn from this chapter when it comes to addressing critics in our lives. Even more so, there are cautions we need to remember in the midst of criticism. Our words, along with our heart motivations, matter. We will see God's heart shine through the words of Jesus. Despite criticism, Jesus is not deterred from His purpose. He addresses the critics while keeping to the task at hand: healing the sick, proclaiming God's kingdom to come, and extending the love of God to all who would receive. There will always be human critics in this world, but the only opinion that matters the most is God's. Are you obeying Him and honoring Him? That was Jesus' focus and should be ours too.

RECEIVING God's Word

Open in Prayer
Read Matthew 12

EXPERIENCING God's Word

Experience 1: Matthew 12:1–21

1. Read Matthew 12:1–2. It was the Sabbath, and Jesus and His disciples were traveling through a grain field. There are Pharisees nearby. What do they accuse the disciples of doing and why?

2. In Matthew 12:3–5 Jesus responds to His critics by citing an Old Testament example from David's life in 1 Samuel 21:2–6. Read the verses in 1 Samuel and describe how David's actions, as well as the disciples', were justified.

3. Read Matthew 12:5. Jesus points out that the Pharisees are accusing the disciples of violating the law but excuse the priest's actions on the Sabbath. Jesus points out their flawed thinking. What is it?

4. Jesus continues to respond to the Pharisees' accusations in verses 6–8. How does His reply speak to His authority and character?

   a. Jesus makes a very bold statement in verse 6 when He says that He is greater than the temple. Why would this statement have upset the Jewish leadership even though it was a truthful statement?

b. Matthew 12:7 says, "I desire mercy and not sacrifice." Jesus quoted this from Hosea 6:6. We saw Jesus say this same phrase back in Matthew 9:13. If the Pharisees had understood what this meant, they would not have found the disciples or Jesus guilty. Why? In your own words explain the meaning of Jesus statement.

5. Read Matthew 12:9–10. When Jesus enters a synagogue, He encounters a man with a withered hand. How do the Pharisees use this man to accuse Jesus?

   a. Jesus responds in verses 11–13 by addressing the value of life, the trap of legalism, and the power of restoration. From these verses, explain Jesus' response in these areas.

6. Read Matthew 12:14–15. The Pharisees are angered and plot how they can destroy Jesus. How does Jesus' response show His lack of concern regarding their evil plot?

7. In Matthew 12:16–21 a great multitude of people are following Jesus, and He is healing them. He asks them not to reveal His identity. In doing so, He fulfills the Old Testament prophecy regarding the Messiah. Read Isaiah 42:1–4. List all you learn about Jesus from this prophecy.

   a. Through these verses in Matthew and Isaiah, who is going to benefit from the Jewish rejection? How do these verses demonstrate God's foreknowledge of Jesus' rejection?

Experience 2: Matthew 12:22–37

1. Read Matthew 12:22–23. Another man is brought to Jesus. The Pharisees likely believed this man's situation was hopeless because they believed in order to be in authority over a demon, you first had to know its name. Describe the condition of the man brought to Jesus, what Jesus did for him, and the response of those who witness Jesus' care for this man.

   a. Read 2 Samuel 7:12–13. God made a covenant with David. What does God tell David will come through him and be established forever?

2. Read Matthew 12:24–26. After the Pharisees hear of Jesus' healing, they accuse Jesus of being a mere man under the influence of Satan in verse 24. Jesus unveils His omnipotence in His response to the accusations. Use verses 25–26 to describe how Jesus tears down their argument with logic.

3. In Matthew 12:27 Jesus takes the accusation against Him and turns it upon them. What does He say, and how does He describe the judgment that will come upon them?

4. In verse 28, what declaration does Jesus make?

5. Read Matthew 12:29–30. Who is the "strong man," and how does Jesus overcome him?

   a. What bold statement does Jesus proclaim regarding the Pharisees' allegiance?

6. According to Merriam-Webster, *blasphemy* is "the act of insulting or showing contempt to something sacred." The blasphemy of the Holy Spirit is "the outward rejection of the ministry and work of Jesus Christ." Given that understanding, read Matthew 12:31–32. What is Jesus accusing the Pharisees of that has eternal consequences?

7. Read Matthew 12:33–37. Jesus goes on to teach the clear distinction between good and evil by using a fruit tree. The "fruit" seen in a person's life gives testimony to what is on the inside of every person. Jesus says in verse 33 that fruit will either be good or evil.

   a. In verses 34–35, what does Jesus call the Pharisees and why?

   b. How do our words give testimony to others?

   c. How do our words impact judgment to come?

Experience 3: Matthew 12:38–50

1. The scribes and Pharisees ask Jesus for a sign that shows who He is. Interestingly, they call Him "teacher." Read Matthew 12:38–39. Jesus calls them an "evil and adulterous" generation. Describe what he meant by the evil and adulterous seek a sign.

2. Read Matthew 12:39–42. What two signs will be given to prove to that generation that Jesus is the Messiah?

   a. Compare and contrast the illustration Jesus makes between Himself and Jonah as well as the Ninevites and the Pharisees.

   b. Read 1 Kings 10:1–9 to learn more about the queen of Sheba. Why did she go to King Solomon, and what resulted? How is she an example to the religious leaders?

   c. According to verses 41 and 42, how will both the Ninevites and the queen of the south condemn the religious leaders?

"Greater light requires greater judgment. Both Nineveh and the queen of the south repented even though they had a lesser light shining in their midst. The rejection of the greater light by the religious leaders was indefensible." (David Guzik, Enduring Word Commentary, www.blueletterbible.org)

3. Read Matthew 12:43–45. Throughout this chapter Jesus has pointed out the wickedness in the hearts of the religious leaders as well as their rejection of Him. According to these verses, where does an unclean spirit make its home?

   a. If rejection persists, what is the end result of the person living in rejection and wickedness according to these verses?

4. Read Jesus' account with His earthly family in Matthew 12:46–50. Who does Jesus say is His family and why?

   a. How does Jesus' last statement about the family of God summarize the whole chapter?

5. Write a short description of Jesus as the King of Kings from what you learned in this chapter.

 **ACTING on God's Word**

In Matthew 12 we read about the criticisms that were assigned to Jesus and His ministry. First, Jesus and His disciples were accused of breaking the Sabbath's rules. Later, Jesus healed a demon-possessed man, and the Pharisees suspected He accomplished this miracle with the help of Beelzebub. Finally, the religious leadership wanted proof of Jesus' divinity through requesting a sign from Him. With each encounter Jesus responded to His critics the same way; He applied truth over the situation.

When we minister in Jesus' name, it would be wise to anticipate some measure of criticism since we will never please all of the people all of the time. We live in a fallen world and minister to fallen people. Therefore, they will likely respond out of their sin nature sooner or later. Because Jesus left us with a written account of how He dealt with His critics, we have a guide for how to respond when this happens to us.

1. Matthew 12:3 begins with "Have you not read…." The first way Jesus opposed the lies brought against Him was by using the truth contained in scripture to expose His critics' mistaken conclusions. Why is scripture the most important tool to use when opposing a critic?

    a. How have you applied scripture over a circumstance in the past? What resulted?

2. Jesus used a logical explanation in Matthew 12:22–30 to describe how the Pharisees' explanation of His power to perform miracles was severely flawed. Why is it important to try the strategy of logic with some critics?

   a. Has this tactic been effective when dealing with a critical person? Explain.

3. In Matthew 12:33–35 Jesus used the example of how the fruit in someone's life is evidence of what is developing within their heart. When a critic comes against you, how can you use the fruit, or lack thereof, to capture an idea of what is happening in one's heart?

   a. How might this help you when trying to understand if there is any merit to their criticism?

4. In Matthew 12:15 Jesus withdrew from the area where the Pharisees were plotting against Him and ministered elsewhere. Based on this, are there times when it is wise to withdraw from an area and work elsewhere? Why or why not?

 **DELIGHTING** in God's Word

From Matthew 12, how has the Lord prompted you to pray?

Write a verse from the chapter that God has spoken to your heart.

Close in Prayer

"The one thing I ask of the Lord - the thing I seek most - is to live in the house of the Lord all the days of my life, delighting in the Lord's perfections and meditating in his temple." Psalm 27:4

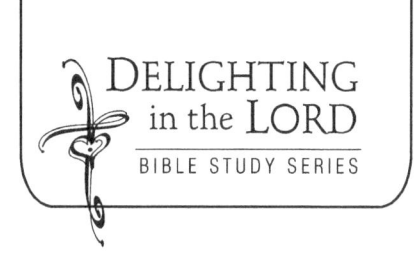

WEEK 4

THE KING TEACHES IN PARABLES ABOUT HIS KINGDOM

Matthew 13

As we open up Matthew chapter 13, we find Jesus teaching through the use of parables. Many consider this chapter one of the most important chapters in this Gospel because it unfolds the mysteries of the kingdom of heaven. However, these mysteries can be misinterpreted without a proper understanding of the difference between the kingdom of heaven and the kingdom of God. The kingdom of heaven describes the millennial kingdom, which is still to come, and God will establish it at His appointed time. This will occur after the Lord's second coming, and there will be a new heaven and a new earth. The kingdom of God is simply God's reign over earthly Christians in the present age. Through the use of parables, Jesus reveals the secrets of His kingdom to come.

The word parable means "to place beside." In this chapter Jesus takes spiritual lessons and places them beside earthly examples in order to illustrate a point (and there is usually just one point per parable). The parables may seem simple, but they are profound. There are seven parables found in chapter 13. In the first four parables Jesus is speaking to the multitudes, and in the last three He instructs His disciples. Divine revelation was needed to understand the parables.

If you consult various commentators regarding the parables, you will likely get many assorted interpretations as to what each commentator believes the text is trying to convey. Therefore, Stacy and I have been very careful to give you information in this lesson that is consistent with the whole counsel of God. There is a name for this type of approach, and it is called using expositional constancy. This simply means allowing scripture to explain scripture. For example, since Jesus tells us that a field represents the world, then every time a field is included in a parable it represents the world. Without the use of expositional constancy, we might draw incorrect conclusions, especially when studying parables.

The lesson ahead is one of the longer in our study of Matthew, but we believe you will come away with a rich understanding of what Jesus wanted people to know about the kingdom of heaven. His message is one that is both exciting and sobering. May God give you ears to hear and a heart to understand the truths presented in this chapter.

RECEIVING God's Word

Open in Prayer
Read Matthew 13

EXPERIENCING God's Word

Experience 1: Matthew 13:1–23

1. Read Matthew 13:1–2. Wherever Jesus went, multitudes came and gathered around Him. What did Jesus do in order to be able to communicate better with the audience?

2. Read the parable Jesus spoke in Matthew 13:3–9 and His application in Matthew 13:18–23. Use these verses to fill in the chart below.

Who is the person or object being described?	Spiritual Application
The sower (v.3)	

cont'd on next page

Delighting in the King of Kings

Who is the person or object being described?	Spiritual Application
The seed (v.4–8; 18–23)	
The wayside (v.4, 19)	
The birds (v.4, 19)	
Stony soil (v.5, 20)	
The sun (v.6, 21)	
No roots (v.6, 21)	
Thorny soil (v. 7, 22)	
Choked out (v. 7, 22)	
Good ground (v. 8, 23)	
Yielded a crop (v. 8, 23)	

3. Does the seed or the soil remain constant in the parables in Matthew 13:3–9 and 18–23? How is this like Jesus and His message of salvation?

4. Read Matthew 13:10–11. The disciples question why Jesus spoke in parables. What does Jesus tell the disciples they have received? Who is the "them" in verse 11 and what have they not received?

5. In verse 12 we see there are those who have understanding and those who don't. Describe what happens to both sets of people concerning the teachings Jesus gives through parables.

6. Jesus gives His reasoning for using parables for those who have not received in verse 13. What does He say?

7. Read Matthew 13:14–15. Jesus quotes Isaiah 6:9–10 in these verses to show that those who have not received the mysteries of the kingdom have fulfilled the prophecy of long ago. How does He describe those who have not received His mysteries and the consequences that have resulted?

8. Jesus identifies His disciples as being "blessed" in verses 16–17. How are these men blessed?

Experience 2: Matthew 13:24–43

1. Read Matthew 13:24–30 and Matthew 13:36–43. Use these verses to fill in the chart below. Some of the answers will be the same as the answers in the previous chart because of expositional constancy.

Who is the person or object being described?	Spiritual Application
The good sower (v. 24, 37)	
The enemy sower (v.25, 39)	

Who is the person or object being described?	Spiritual Application
The wheat seed (v.24, 37–38)	
The tare seed (v.25, 38, 40)	
The field (v.24, 38)	
His enemy (v.28, 39)	
The harvest (v.30, 39, 41–43)	

2. When were the tares sown into the field? (vs. 25) What does this suggest about the time when the enemy strikes?

3. When can the grasses (wheat and tares) be distinguished from one another? (vs. 26)

4. Why doesn't the owner of the field want the servants to pull up the tares in the field according to verses 27–29?

5. We read in verse 30 that when the field is harvested, the wheat and the tares are separated. Where will the wheat go, and what happens to the tares?

   a. Read Revelation 20:11–15 and 21:1–5. Based on these verses, where is the "barn" for the believer in Jesus Christ, and where is the "fire" for the person who refuses to believe in Jesus Christ?

6. Jesus teaches two more parables regarding the kingdom of heaven in Matthew 13:31–33. When you read them, please be sure to use expositional constancy with the answers you provide.

   a. Read Matthew 13:31. A mustard seed is being planted. Who is planting the seed, and what does the field represent?

b. The seed that was planted in the previous verse grows in verse 32. Describe the outcome.

c. Read Matthew 13:33. Please keep in mind that normally yeast symbolizes something evil or unclean (Matthew 16:12 and 1 Corinthians 5:8). Yeast is added to flour to make it rise and grow. What does this signify about some of the growth that had developed within the kingdom community?

7. How is the message Jesus gives in Matthew 13:34–35 similar to the words of Asaph in Psalm 78:1–2?

Experience 3: Matthew 13:44–58

1. Read Matthew 13:44–46. In order to understand this parable, we must keep the consistency of God's word in mind. We did not sell anything, nor did we buy anything to obtain our salvation. Salvation is a free gift extended to all. With this in mind, answer the following questions:

    a. According to verse 44, who is the "man" in this parable? What did He do? Who is the "treasure?"

b. Who is the "merchant," and who is the "great pearl" in verses 45 and 46?

2. Read Matthew 13:47–50. Then answer the questions below.

   a. From verses 47–48, when will the fish be divided?

   b. In verse 49 when will the net be brought on shore? What does this represent?

   c. What sober warning is given in verse 50?

3. Read Matthew 25:41. Who was hell created for?

4. Read Matthew 13:51–53. Jesus' disciples say they have understood what He has taught them. Jesus follows up with a parable regarding a householder. Who is the homeowner? What are the new treasures, and what are the old treasures?

   a. What responsibility does the homeowner have regarding what has been entrusted to him?

5. Read Matthew 13:54. Where does Jesus travel to, and why are the occupants of the town astonished at Jesus?

6. The people are trying to put together Jesus' lineage in verses 55–57. Why were they offended by Him? How did Jesus reply to their offense?

7. According to Matthew 13:58, how much power did Jesus demonstrate in this town and why?

8. Write a short description of Jesus as the King of Kings from what you learned in this chapter.

ACTING on God's Word

After several hours of writing the Experiencing questions, I (Brenda) took a break on the porch of the house where we were staying to write Matthew. My brain was full, and to be quite frank, I was feeling a bit overwhelmed. I closed my eyes and asked the Lord, "What is the big takeaway here? How can we apply these parables to our lives today?" And as I opened my Bible and read the chapter again, the most remarkable discovery occurred. I have given you what came to me below as headings, and then would like you to consider how to apply them to your own life.

1. Soil can represent a person's heart condition

   Based on what you learned from the parable of the soils, explain which type of soil represents your heart toward the Lord. Is there a need for any change? If so, describe it below.

2. Wheat seeds can represent believing Jesus, and tare seeds can represent believing in false teachers

   Based on what you learned from the parable of the wheat and the tares, have you put your trust in Christ alone, or are you trusting in something else? Explain.

3. Leaven can represent how evil flourishes

Is there sin in your life that needs to be confessed? Leaven in the parable defiles the entire loaf of bread. How do you see this truth operating in your life?

4. Mankind can be represented as pearls and a great treasure

For a moment, consider what it cost Jesus to redeem your life from the debt of sin you owed. Jesus thought you and I were worth it. Write a few sentences of gratitude to Jesus for giving His all on your behalf.

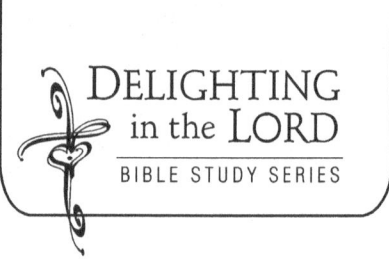

5. A dragnet can represent how all of mankind will eventually be collected up to stand before God

Someday each of us will stand before God and give account for our choices made upon this earth. There is one question which will determine your eternal destiny, and that is, "Did you put your faith in Jesus Christ as your Lord and Savior?" How will you answer this question? If you have never done this, please refer to the Delighting in My Salvation page found in the beginning of this book.

6. A householder can represent a person who has heard the Gospel

If you have put your faith in Jesus Christ, you are responsible to share that wonderful news with others. In what ways are you actively telling others about Jesus? How are you using the treasures you have been entrusted with?

 **D** DELIGHTING in God's Word

From Matthew 13, how has the Lord prompted you to pray?

Write a verse from the chapter that God has spoken to your heart.

Close in Prayer

"The one thing I ask of the Lord - the thing I seek most - is to live in the house of the Lord all the days of my life, delighting in the Lord's perfections and meditating in his temple." Psalm 27:4

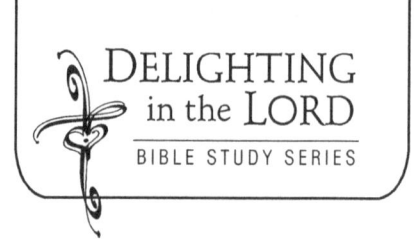

WEEK 5
THE KING PROVIDES FOR HIS PEOPLE
Matthew 14

In 2008, my already handicapped mother was hit by a car while visiting her sister in Virginia. It was late in the afternoon on Thanksgiving Day when she decided to walk off the turkey dinner she enjoyed hours before. As she walked through her sister's townhouse streets, sun glare blinded a driver, and my mom was hit from behind. Suffering a brain bleed, my mom had to go through months of hospital stays and rehab. It was in the rehab hospital where I (Stacy) was first confronted with the overwhelming need and deep suffering of mankind.

We all know that hospitals hold the physically sick. But where there is physical disease or disability, there are often deep needs that go beyond the physical. I spent each day with my mother at the rehab hospital where I would see the needs of hurting people all around me. I watched God provide for the needs of other patients, as well as my mother's needs, over and over again. Impossible situations became possible and even manageable. From opening doors in facilities and putting certain nurses over her care, to financial provision and even ministering to her emotional needs. My sisters and I would read to Mom from a daily devotional she loved, and day after day the words of Jesus met my mom in her fears and uncertainties. Jesus sees our needs and addresses each one in His most perfect ways.

In Matthew 14 we see the King of Kings meet the needs of people in impossible situations. We will see Jesus feed 5,000 people with five loaves of bread and two small fish. Jesus' disciples wanted to send the people away who were there to hear Jesus. The disciples wanted them to fend for themselves in their hunger. But Jesus had other plans. As we will see, He has the people sit down on the grassy field and He multiplies the food in front of the disciples' eyes. The need of the people was His need. Their need mattered to Him. Psalm 145:16 says, "You open your hand and satisfy the desire of every living thing." Jesus had a wonderful lesson to teach His disciples about human need and compassion. We can easily turn our heads away from people's needs, yet Jesus presses into those needs.

After the miraculous feeding, Jesus will enter into His disciples' fears and uncertainties. The Sea of Galilee should have been a comfortable and familiar place for the disciples. Many of them were fishermen and had spent many hours in boats on that very sea. However, this time the sea became a place of fear. It was dark and turbulent, and they must have felt

alone knowing that Jesus was on the mountain praying and not in the boat with them. Fear often grips us in places of need, uncertainty, and difficulty as it did with Peter in Matthew 14. Once again, Jesus shows Peter and the disciples that He provides what they need in all circumstances. In this case, He provided peace in a storm and made tumultuous seas feel as if they were calm.

God says in Isaiah 41:10, "Fear not, for I am with you. Be not dismayed for I am your God. I will strengthen you. Yes, I will help you. I will uphold you with my righteous right hand." That is all it takes with God, the lifting of His hand as He extends Himself to each of us, providing for our needs in each moment. I don't know what need you have as you open this chapter. But rest assured, God sees your need and desires to provide what is needed in your specific circumstances.

R RECEIVING God's Word

Open in Prayer
Read Matthew 14

E EXPERIENCING God's Word

Experience 1: Matthew 14:1–21

1. Herod the tetrarch, known as Herod Antipas, was ruler over Palestine, Galilee, and Perea from 4 BC to AD 39. Read Matthew 14:1–5. Keep in mind that John the Baptist has already died, and there is a flashback included in these verses. As Herod hears about the works of Jesus, He thinks that Jesus is a resurrected John the Baptist. From these verses, describe what Herod had done to John the Baptist and why.

    a. What reason is given as to why Herod didn't kill John the Baptist in verse 5? How does this information reinforce Herod's conclusion about Jesus?

2. Read Matthew 14:6–11. How was John the Baptist killed?

    a. Describe sin's effect upon King Herod, Herodias, Herodias' daughter, and John the Baptist.

3. How do the disciples show great care for John the Baptist as well as Jesus' relationship with John according to verse 12?

4. Read Matthew 14:13. What did Jesus do upon hearing of John's death? What does this say about the grief that Jesus was undoubtedly experiencing?

5. From verses 13–14, how was Jesus' time alone interrupted, and how did He responded in the midst of the interruption?

6. As evening descended, Jesus' disciples show great care for Jesus' physical and emotional well-being. Read Matthew 14:15. What do they suggest to Jesus?

   a. Were Jesus' disciples compassionate to the multitudes gathered? Explain.

7. In verses 16–17 Jesus wanted to feed the people gathered. The disciples were concerned about the logistics. What was Jesus' solution, and what complications did the disciples foresee with Jesus' solution?

8. Read John's account of this interaction in John 6:5–9. John tells us this was a test. What was Jesus testing with His disciples? What did He want them to see and understand? Keep in mind that Jesus knew He would soon be leaving them, and they would continue the work of the Lord on earth. At this point the disciples had no understanding of this. Look back at Matthew 13:10–13 for help with this question if needed.

9. Read Matthew 14:18–21 and answer the following questions:

   a. What does Jesus do? Describe the meal Jesus provided.

   b. What do the multitudes do?

   c. What do the disciples do?

   d. How did the people feel after the meal?

> "About 5,000 men were fed on this occasion, plus women and children, perhaps 15,000 to 20,000 in all." (*Bible Knowledge Commentary*, pg. 54)

10. How did Jesus use the feeding of the 5,000 to demonstrate spiritual principles? What were the principles?

11. Read Philippians 4:19 and Ephesians 3:20. How do these verses support the miracle in Matthew 14?

Experience 2: Matthew 14:22–36

1. Read Matthew 14:22–23. Where is Jesus? Where are the disciples, and what are they doing?

2. Matthew 14:24–25 tells us the disciples' boat was in the middle of the sea being tossed by the waves and wind. In the fourth watch of the night, Jesus came to the disciples. The fourth watch would have been between 3:00 and 6:00 AM. John 6:19 tells us that the disciples had been rowing for 3-4 miles before Jesus came to them. Why would Jesus allow this time to elapse?

3. The disciples see Jesus coming to them in verse 26. How does Jesus meet them, and how do they respond?

4. In verse 27 Jesus speaks into the fears of His disciples by speaking three things. They are listed below. After each point, tell why Jesus would respond this way in their tumultuous circumstances. How does Jesus bring calmness by saying these things?

   - "Be of good cheer (courage)"

   - "It is I"

   - "Do not be afraid"

5. Read Matthew 14:28. Peter, wanting Jesus to reveal His identity, calls out to Him and asks if he could join Him on the water. This scenario could have played out much differently. Peter could have waited for Jesus to get in the boat. He could have stepped out of the boat the minute he saw Jesus. He could have hidden in the boat. What conclusions can you draw from Peter's request to Jesus regarding his trust in Jesus?

Delighting in the King of Kings

6. In Matthew 14:29 Jesus gives a one word command to Peter, and Peter obeys. Peter does three things in verses 29–30. What are they, and how does each action exhibit fear or faith?

   a. Faith has been described as a single-minded focus on God, and fear as a divided focus. From these verses, how do you see faith and fear operating at different times in the same person?

   b. What did faith do for Peter? What did fear do for him?

7. Read Matthew 14:31. How does Jesus provide for Peter in his cry for help?

8. Read Matthew 14:32–33. Overall, what was Jesus trying to teach Peter and the disciples through this storm?

   a. What was their response to Jesus when He and Peter got back in the boat? How are worship and faith tied together?

9. Finish the chapter by reading Matthew 14:34–36. Jesus and His disciples enter Gennesaret, and many sick people come to Jesus for healing. These verses say that Jesus made them "perfectly well." What did the people do? What does this say about their faith?

10. Write a short description of Jesus as the King of Kings from what you learned in this chapter.

 **A** ACTING on God's Word

There have been so many times in my (Stacy's) life where God has met my needs in unexpected, exact, and what has seemed like miraculous ways. Years ago, I took a part-time job selling Pampered Chef to help meet our family's financial needs while staying home with our children. Each month I needed to make $500. In the year I sold kitchen gadgets, I made exactly what was needed and sometimes a bit more. God often stretched my faith as I trusted Him, but He always provided for the need. Over the years I have received unexpected refund checks at an exact time I've needed money for expenses. I've had dinners show up at my doorstep in times of trials. During a fragile time with our 4th son, who was born with a genetic deformity, I watched God provide church families who offered to watch my other children so I could care for Joshua. Even more, I've watched the Lord meet my emotional and spiritual needs again and again. My Bible is like a journal with dates marking verses where God provided what I needed on dark and despairing days. He is so faithful to His people!

1. In Matthew 14 Jesus provided for the hungry when He fed the 5,000. Jesus not only met the people's needs, but He provided more than enough. From Matthew 14, recall how Jesus' provision exceeded the needs of the hungry.

   a. Give an example of a time in your life when God provided for you or your family in extravagant and miraculous ways exceeding a need.

2. When Jesus fed the 5,000, He wanted to show them His power to provide. He could have sent them away to fend for themselves, but instead He provided for them that made it clear the provision came from Him. Describe a time when you could have met your own need, but God made it clear you were to rely on His power and timing for that need.

3. After Jesus fed the hungry, they were full. How does Jesus' provision leave you full?

4. When a storm arose on the Sea of Galilee and the disciples were in the middle of the sea in the midst of the storm, how did Jesus meet their need?

   a. When was the last time you cried out in fear to Jesus? Describe how He met you in your fear and gave you courage.

   b. If you struggle with fear, how does this chapter encourage you with God's provision?

5. Lastly, Jesus calmed the storm, causing the wind to stop blowing and the waves to stop tumbling over the boat. Matthew 14:32 says the storm stopped when Peter and Jesus got back in the boat. What spiritual application can you make regarding God's provision?

 **DELIGHTING in God's Word**

From Matthew 14, how has the Lord prompted you to pray?

Write a verse from the chapter that God has spoken to your heart.

Close in Prayer

"The one thing I ask of the Lord - the thing I seek most - is to live in the house of the Lord all the days of my life, delighting in the Lord's perfections and meditating in his temple." Psalm 27:4

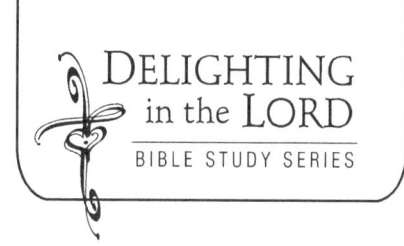

WEEK 6
THE KING LIFTS BURDENS

Matthew 15

Calvary Chapel Chester Springs, like many churches, has a prayer chain. I (Brenda) am one of the people who has signed up to receive the prayer needs so that I can lift them before the Lord. The requests come to me via e-mail, and I probably get eight to ten prayer requests a week to pray over. Often when I read the burdens the body of Christ is facing, my heart breaks. With empathy, I pray over the needs. I must admit, however, there are days when I receive the prayer chain e-mails and I am overcome by the content I read. The circumstances seem insurmountable, and they often involve broken relationships, sickness, financial ruin, addictions or a desperate plea for God's wisdom. I feel so helpless when I consider the hardships and think about the stresses and burdens my brothers and sisters in Christ are facing. I want so badly to remove their pain, but I know the best thing I can do is pray. I turn to the only One who can do abundantly more than I can ask or imagine (Ephesians 3:10), and I ask Him to help them.

In Matthew 15 the people of Jesus' day were also facing needs beyond what man could do to help them. There was unbelief within the religious leadership. Among the multitudes, many were demon-possessed, lame, blind, mute, maimed, and hungry. Everywhere Jesus looked, there was brokenness and pain. The needs were great, but He has always been greater. He took each situation, one at a time, and applied His sovereign touch upon it. Sometimes that took the form of a question or a rebuke, but most of the time it was His divine intervention which resulted in an immediate healing.

As you begin your study time, perhaps there are some burdens you have which seem overwhelming and seem impossible. Be encouraged! You are about to read how the Lord who loves you, ministered to the brokenhearted while He was on earth. He knows what is weighing you down. He is ever ready and able to help you just as He did when He was walking around Jerusalem, Tyre, Sidon, and the shores of Galilee. Those who came to Jesus, truly seeking His help, went away full and free. Listen for His gentle voice as you read your Bible and look for His peace to lift your burdened heart.

RECEIVING God's Word

Open in Prayer
Read Matthew 15

EXPERIENCING God's Word

Experience 1: Matthew 15:1–20

1. Read Matthew 15:1–2. Describe what the disciples did to offend the scribes and Pharisees.

2. Jesus points out the sin of the scribes and the Pharisees in verses 3–4. They are using their Jewish tradition to cover up their disobedience to God's commands. According to verse 4, what command are they disobeying?

    a. Jesus could have easily shut down the Pharisees and scribes by telling them their oral tradition was invalid. But instead, Jesus addresses their question with a question of His own. Why would Jesus have entertained their questions?

3. Read Matthew 15:5–6. Describe the Jewish tradition that the scribes and Pharisees are upholding over God's law.

> The Jews believed and still believe (at least, the orthodox) in a written law and in an oral law. This they founded upon Exodus 34:27 and taught that while Moses wrote down a law another oral law was given to him and that this oral law was handed down from generation to generation. It is believed by them that Moses received both the written and the oral law on Mount Sinai. They placed the oral law above the written law. Circumstances, however, forced them to commit the oral law to writing, which was done in the Talmud, from which we can learn all the ridiculous paraphrases and wicked additions to the law the ancients had made under the plea that it was given by God. (*The Gospel of Matthew, An Exposition* by Arno C. Gaebelein, pg. 325)

4. Read Matthew 15:7–9. What does Jesus call the scribes and Pharisees? Why would Jesus quote Isaiah 29:13 as His answer back to them?

5. Jesus calls the disciples to Himself in verses 10–11. He tells them they need to grasp the point that He is making. What is it, and how does this go against what the scribes and Pharisees teach?

6. In Matthew 15:12 the disciples ask Jesus if He realized that the Pharisees were offended by what He said. Why was this a ridiculous question?

7. Read Matthew 15:13–14. What does Jesus say about the leadership of the Pharisees and the impact they are having upon their followers?

8. Read Matthew 15:15–20. Peter asks Jesus to explain what He meant when He said, "Not what goes into the mouth defiles a man but what comes out of the mouth, this defiles a man." In your own words, summarize what Jesus told Peter was the essence of our defilement. Is defilement outward or inward? Explain.

a. Peter is struggling to understand what Jesus is teaching in verses 16–17. As a Jew, he grew up with the same traditions as the leadership but has also, according to Matthew 13:11, been given the mysteries of heaven. With this in mind, why do you think it was so hard for him to understand what Jesus was saying?

Experience 2: Matthew 15:21–39

1. Read Matthew 15:21–22. Jesus travels with His disciples to the region of Tyre and Sidon. These are Gentile cities that had come under God's judgment. Who does Jesus encounter?

    a. Describe how this woman approaches Jesus. What can you infer about her faith from her words?

2. Read Matthew 15:23–25. Here we see the response of Jesus to the woman, the disciples' response to Jesus, and the woman's response to Jesus. What do you notice about each of their responses?

   - Jesus to the woman:

   - Disciples to Jesus:

   - The woman to Jesus:

3. Jesus responds to her plea for help once again in verse 26. In His response, who are the "children," and who are "the little dogs?"

   a. Jesus' response in verses 24 and 26 can seem harsh at first glance. Based on what you've learned so far in Matthew, who was Jesus sent to minister to first? How might His response coincide with carrying out God's plan? We are told in verse 21 that Jesus went to a Gentile city. We don't know if He went there purposefully as the text does not include that detail. However, this is something to consider in the interactions Jesus has with this woman.

4. Read Matthew 15:27. The Gentile woman pleads with Jesus once again, calling Him Lord and Master. How do you see her humility coming forth with her request for "crumbs?"

5. Jesus answers her plea with an honorable accolade that He has not used with anyone else. What stands out to Jesus regarding this woman in verse 28?

    a. What does Jesus do for this woman?

6. Read Matthew 15:29–31. Jesus went up on a mountain, and the multitudes joined Him there. Describe the scene and what occurred through Jesus' power. How did the people thank Him?

7. Back in Matthew 14:13–21 we learned how Jesus fed 5,000 people. Now we have a similar miracle recorded. List the similarities and differences you observe from the account in chapter 14 versus the one here in Matthew 15:32–39.

    a. Matthew 15:32 says that the multitudes were with Jesus for three days. He doesn't want them to be sent away hungry. Why might three days be a significant number?

b. Read Exodus 16:4. What did God do for the children of Israel in the wilderness? How does the disciples' question in Matthew 15:33 seem silly in light of what they know and have witnessed about God and His care for His people?

8. Write a short description of Jesus as the King of Kings from what you learned in this chapter.

 **ACTING on God's Word**

None of us are exempt from burdens in this life. Burdens come in all shapes and sizes, but we all carry them, just with different names. The word *burden* in the New Testament denotes the troubles we have in this life. Those troubles can be heavy. They can weigh us down as well as be a constant distraction. We looked at four different types of people in Matthew 15. Each person or group of people had burdens that were weighing them down. Some knew they were weighed down, and some didn't. Let's look at these people and learn from what Jesus did for them in the midst of their difficulties.

Delighting in the King of Kings

1. <u>The Jewish Religious Leadership (Scribes and Pharisees)—Matthew 15:1–20</u>
   Burden: Religious Traditions & Legalism

   a. How can religious traditions be a burden?

   b. Have you ever been weighed down with the burden of religious traditions? Explain.

   c. What was Jesus' answer to this burden as seen in Matthew 15? How can you apply this same answer to this burden in your life or for a loved one?

2. The Gentile Woman—Matthew 15:21–28
   Burden: Daughter who was severely demon-possessed; mental health issues

   a. How can mental health issues be a burden?

   b. Have you ever been weighed down with a burden caused by mental health issues? Explain.

   c. In Matthew 15 we saw this woman call out to Jesus, worship Him, and humble herself before Him. 1 Peter 5:6–7 says, "Therefore humble yourself under the mighty hand of God, that He may exalt you in due time, casting all your care upon Him, for He cares for you." The woman did this, and we need to learn from her example. She had Jesus right in front of her. We can approach Him through prayer. When we don't pray about burdensome needs, we are basically

telling God, "We've got this." This is not what God intends. Write out a prayer to the Lord below calling out to Him, worshipping Him, and humbling yourself before Him in your need.

3. The Multitudes of Sick People—Matthew 15:29–31

   Burden: Physical Disease

   a. How can physical disease be a burden?

   b. Have you ever been weighed down with a burden caused by physical disease? Explain.

    c. In Matthew 15 the physically ill came to Jesus for physical healing. When they were healed, they glorified God. If you are physically ill, God has allowed this to accomplish something in you and through you for His glory. 2 Corinthians 12:7–10 tells us Paul had a thorn in his flesh. We don't know what it was, but he repeatedly asked God to take it from him. God didn't. He told Paul that His grace was sufficient. There are burdens we need to bear with God's grace, and there are burdens God didn't intend for us to bear. How do we accept the burdens God has for us and still live weightless lives?

4. <u>The Hungry—Matthew 15:32–39</u>
   Burden: Hunger

   a. How can hunger be a burden?

   b. Have you or someone you know ever experienced the burden of hunger? Explain.

c. In Matthew 15 Jesus fed the multitude. They came hungry and left full. Do you have a burden for the hungry? Maybe God would have you minister in His name to these people. There are many ministries that serve the hungry. Galatians 6:2 tells us to "bear one another's burdens." How can you actively walk this out?

DELIGHTING in God's Word

From Matthew 15, how has the Lord prompted you to pray?

Write a verse from the chapter that God has spoken to your heart.

Close in Prayer

"The one thing I ask of the Lord - the thing I seek most - is to live in the house of the Lord all the days of my life, delighting in the Lord's perfections and meditating in his temple." Psalm 27:4

WEEK 7
THE KING REINFORCES SPIRITUAL PRINCIPLES
Matthew 16

From the time my sons (Stacy's) were in late elementary school, they all played football. We have had our share of football injuries, but we've never had to deal with a concussion. That is until early October of 2018, when my fourteen-year-old son Jed suffered a football concussion. Jed endured three months of therapy and rehab. During this time of healing, he missed out on a lot of the "normal" in his life, and he struggled in many physical ways. As symptoms dissipated and day-to-day activities resumed, we thought the concussion was a thing of the past. As March approached, so did the lacrosse season. Lacrosse is his passion. As he took to the lacrosse field, he was ready to go; gear on and lacrosse stick in hand. However, within an hour of running, throwing, and drill work, his head began to pound, the glare of the field lights blinded him, and he had to leave the practice. As I write this in May, he still is not symptom-free. All of his concussion symptoms were reignited with lacrosse. Life for him has come to a standstill of sorts. It has been so difficult to watch him suffer in this way.

As Jed and I have had some deep conversations about his physical injury, I have felt prompted by God to press into the spiritual aspects of this injury. Having gone through many physical trials of my own, I am sensitive to the fact that God wants to use the physical to teach us deep spiritual lessons. Often, our physical circumstances can be so all-encompassing that we neglect the things of God. We push through or try to understand why things are happening as they are. Sometimes pride hinders our spiritual eyes or brings frustration with God for allowing the suffering. Whatever the reason, I believe God always wants to use our physical situations, or in Jed's case, his concussion, to teach and refine our hearts for God's glory. He has spiritual truths He wants to teach Jed through this difficulty.

If we are willing to listen and learn, Jesus will use our life as a classroom to teach us more of Him.

Some lessons we are told the disciples understood, but some of Jesus' teachings they clearly missed. The physical things kept drawing their eyes and hearts away. Yet, Jesus is so gracious to share His deep spiritual truths for our lives again and again. For the heart that desires Him, Jesus enters right in. Where are your eyes today? Are they focused on your circumstances, or can you look past the circumstance to the cross and let Jesus meet you there?

RECEIVING God's Word

Open in Prayer
Read Matthew 16

EXPERIENCING God's Word

Experience 1: Matthew 16:1–12

For sake of review, following are descriptions of the religious leaders:

Pharisees: Dominant and most influential religious sect who were strict legalists. They believed the Old Testament Law, Prophets and Psalms and wanted to restore the kingdom to the line of David. They lived according to the smallest points of the oral traditions of the elders and scribal law. They believed in angels and the resurrection from the dead. They were not a political party, as they were more interested in the government leaving them alone so they could practice their religion as they intended. They looked and longed for the Messiah.

Sadducees: Made up of the wealthy liberals who were mainly from the priesthood and upper class. They were anti-supernaturalists of Christ's day. The Sadducees were opposed to the Pharisees and their religious traditions. They upheld the written words of the Law of Moses, but opposed the oral tradition observed by the Pharisees. They denied the truth of bodily resurrection, future punishment and reward, and the existence of angels. They collaborated with the Roman government for self-serving interests.

Scribes: A group of professional expounders of the Law, stemming back to the days of Ezra. They were more concerned with the letter of the Law than the spirit of the Law. They knew Scripture but didn't put it into practice.

1. Read Matthew 16:1. The Sadducees and Pharisees unite to test Jesus. What test did they lay before Jesus?

2. Read Matthew 12:38–41. Here the scribes and Pharisees sought a sign from Jesus. Compare and contrast the test in chapter 16 with the test in chapter 12.

> "The word translated sign means much more than simply a miracle or demonstration of power. It means 'a wonder by which one may recognize a person or confirm who he is.' But miracles do not convince people of sin or give a desire for salvation (Luke 16:27–31; John 12:10–11; Acts 14:8–20). Miracles will give confirmation where there is faith, but not where there is willful unbelief." (W. Weirsbe, *Be Loyal*, p. 139–140)

3. Read Jesus' response to the Pharisees and Sadducees in Matthew 16:2–4. What was the main point of His response, and how was the sign of Jonah like a foreshadowing of His future?

4. Read Matthew 16:5–6. Jesus and the disciples cross the Sea of Galilee. The disciples are focused on one thing while Jesus is focused on another. What are the disciples concerned with? What is Jesus concerned with?

5. Read Matthew 16:7–12 and answer the following questions:

   a. Why did the disciples begin reasoning together after Jesus began talking about leaven? (vs.7)

   b. Jesus equates their reasoning with a lack of _____. How does Jesus redirect them back to the point He is trying to make? (vs.8–10)

c. Jesus thoroughly addresses the disciples' distraction of physical things (bread) by pointing them to the spiritual issue. What is the spiritual issue of the Pharisees and Sadducees that He wants them to recognize and understand? (vs.11)

d. They got it in verse 12! Put their revelation in your own words.

Experience 2: Matthew 16:13–20

1. Read Matthew 16:13. What question did Jesus ask His disciples, and why do you think He was asking this question amidst their backdrop? As God, He would have already known their answer, so why did He ask it?

   a. In asking this of His disciples, do you think Jesus was really concerned with what other people thought of Him? Why or why not?

2. The disciples respond to Jesus' question in verse 14. They name three people as possible answers. Following are details on each of the people they used in their response:

- **John the Baptist**—messenger paving the way for Jesus Christ; called for national repentance (Malachi 3:1).

- **Elijah**—Prophet, worker of miracles, devoted to, and sent by God to confront the hostile rulers of the Northern Kingdom who worshipped Baal during 875 BC. According to Malachi 4:5–6, Elijah would announce the coming of "the great and dreadful day of the Lord."

- **Jeremiah**—Known as the "Weeping Prophet" for his great sorrow for the people of Judah as they turned away from the Lord. Jeremiah faithfully proclaimed God's truth and warnings to the people for 40 years in the midst of hostility.

Based on the descriptions of these individuals, how did all of these answers fall short?

3. Jesus begins to make a sharp contrast between what the world says and what the disciples should know. What point was Jesus making here with His disciples?

4. What question does Jesus now ask His disciples in verse 15? Write the question. Why must this question not only be asked of the disciples but also to each of us? What was Jesus looking for in their answer as well as in our answer?

5. We see Peter's two-part answer in verse 16. What did his confession testify to regarding Jesus' identity?

6. Read Matthew 16:17. Jesus responds to Peter's confession. He reveals to Peter that he didn't come upon this knowledge and understanding alone. How was Peter able to give this response and confession? What does this tell you regarding the work of the Holy Spirit in the life of each person?

7. Jesus gives Simon a new name, Peter, in verse 18. What else does Jesus tell Peter in verses 18–19?

8. Much controversy exists among the meaning of verses 18 and 19. Any time a verse is taken outside of context and not looked at within the whole Bible, misinterpretation can occur. Let's look throughout His Word to gain a deeper understanding of what Jesus was saying to Peter. Start by looking at the Aramaic for the words *Peter* and *Rock*. Peter means "Petros," or a stone. It is a proper masculine noun. Rock means "Petra," a rock or large stone. It is a feminine noun this time. Read Matthew 16:18. Who is Jesus building His church upon? What is the foundation?

   a. Read 1 Corinthians 3:11 and write what you learn.

   b. Read Ephesians 2:20–22. What does it say regarding the foundation of the church?

    c. We know that Peter wrote the books of 1 and 2 Peter. Let's read what Peter, through divine inspiration of the Holy Spirit, wrote regarding the church. Read 1 Peter 2:4–7 and note what you learn regarding the church, its members, and the foundation.

9. In Matthew 16:18 the first mention of the church is used in Scripture. It was something brand new for the disciples to understand, and it had not yet begun. The word "church" means "ekklesia." The literal meaning is "a called-out assembly." It refers to the whole body of born-again believers throughout the world. At the end of verse 18, we see a promise from Jesus. What is that promise regarding His church?

10. What authority did Jesus give Peter in verse 19?

> The keys were the badge of authority of the office of the scribes who interpreted the Scriptures to the people (Nehemiah 8:2–8). Every Christian today has the Scriptures and therefore the keys. If we withhold the Word, we "bind on the earth;" if we give the Word, we "loose on earth." No man or individual church has the keys—to the exclusion of all other believers. We have a responsibility today to give out the gospel because it is the only thing that can save people." (J. Vernon McGee, *Thru the Bible Commentary, Volume 35: Matthew Chapters 14–28*, pg. 49)

11. Why do you think Jesus commanded His disciples not to share His identity with others in verse 20?

Experience 3: Matthew 16:21–28

1. Read Matthew 16:21. What four things does Jesus reveal to His disciples? Why would this information be shocking?

2. What does Peter say to Jesus in verse 22?

3. In Matthew 16:23 Jesus calls Peter "Satan" and tells him to get behind Him because he is an offense. Why would Peter's statement cause Jesus to respond strongly?

4. In verses 24–26 Jesus revisits His previous teaching from Matthew 10 regarding taking up our cross and following after Him. In your own words, write what the following statements mean:

- Deny self

- Take up his cross

- Follow Jesus

5. Read Galatians 2:20 and Matthew 16:25. Write the connection you see between these two verses.

6. Read Matthew 16:26. Explain what Jesus was saying about profit and loss.

7. Read Matthew 16:27. Jesus expects works from each believer, and our works will be rewarded. Read James 2:14–17. Will Jesus reward works alone? What kind of works will be rewarded?

8. Read Matthew 16:28. Jesus gives the disciples a foreshadowing. He is alluding to both His death and His transfiguration which will occur in chapter 17. What encouragement does He give the disciples about both suffering and His glorious kingdom to come? Read Romans 8:18 to gain deeper understanding of this principle.

9. Write a short description of Jesus as the King of Kings from what you learned in this chapter.

 **ACTING on God's Word**

Throughout Matthew 16, the people missed the spiritual lessons Jesus was trying to teach them. They allowed their physical circumstances and logical explanations to direct their understanding. Sadly, their response to Jesus' instruction is not a problem isolated to the people of His day, but rather one that has been witnessed throughout the world for thousands of years. However, God desires us to see beyond the natural realm so we can grasp the deeper spiritual things He has for us both in this life and the one to come.

1. The Pharisees and Sadducees wanted Jesus to perform a physical sign from heaven to prove His divinity. Perhaps you can relate to their desire to see a tangible sign. How could this be a snare the enemy might use to weaken your faith and inhibit your trust in God?

2. The disciples realized they left some bread behind after Jesus fed the 4,000. When Jesus said they should take heed of the leaven He witnessed in the Pharisees and Sadducees, the disciples thought Jesus was speaking of the actual bread they forgot to bring with them. Clearly, they missed the deeper significance of Jesus' comment. He wanted them to be aware of their unbelief and hypocrisy. Have you ever

encountered a verse in the Bible, read it, and thought you understood the meaning only to later realize you missed the deeper significance? Write a verse from anywhere in the Bible that you previously did not understand and explain how you interpreted it wrongly.

a. How did your lack of understanding play into your interpretation?

b. How did God show you the deeper significance?

3. Jesus takes the disciples to Caesarea Philippi, a location where many different idols were worshipped. In that physical location, Jesus asked them, "Who do you say that I am?" In essence, am I just another one of these gods, or am I the One and only living God? There are times I think all of us can say we placed our trust in someone or something other than Christ. Why will this always disappoint us and never be enough?

4. At the end of Matthew 16, Jesus explains to the disciples that they must take up their cross, just as He would, and follow Him. Jesus was indicating they must die to their desires and humbly submit to His plans for their life. This would not be easy because the flesh dies hard and our attention is drawn to other things besides Jesus' eternal priorities. How will you combat the lure of your flesh to trust only in what you can see, so that you can discern what the Lord wants to show you spiritually?

 **D** **DELIGHTING** in God's Word

From Matthew 16, how has the Lord prompted you to pray?

Write a verse from the chapter that God has spoken to your heart.

Close in Prayer

"The one thing I ask of the Lord - the thing I seek most - is to live in the house of the Lord all the days of my life, delighting in the Lord's perfections and meditating in his temple." Psalm 27:4

WEEK 8

THE KING'S MAGNIFICENCE

Matthew 17

If you were to close your eyes and picture something magnificent, what would it be?

Would you picture a natural wonder like a dark night sky filled with stars, or would you imagine ocean waves crashing upon the shoreline and then returning to their God-ordained boundaries? Maybe you would picture something from the human realm like a newborn baby, or a complex DNA strand creating new cell information. Perhaps you might picture something man-made, like an ornate ceiling in an Italian cathedral or a complex pyramid sitting alone in a desert.

There are many wonders in this world that capture our attention and are awe-inspiring, but even if we searched the entire world over, we would never find anything more magnificent than Jesus.

In Matthew 17 we will catch a glimpse of Jesus' divinity as His body was transfigured in front of a few of His disciples. Jesus' face became bright like the sun, and His clothes became white like light. Elijah and Moses appeared, and they spoke with Jesus. Then a voice from heaven called out of a bright cloud saying, "This is My beloved Son in whom I am well pleased. Hear Him!" The disciples fell to their faces in fear. The transfiguration was like nothing the disciples had ever witnessed. Each day they spent with Him, He was becoming more and more magnificent. As they cowered in fear upon the ground, Jesus touched them and said, "Arise, and do not be afraid." When they looked up, Jesus had returned to His normal appearance and was alone.

In the text of this lesson, Jesus' transfiguration displays His magnificence, but we will also see Jesus demonstrate His magnificence in other ways as well. Through His divine attributes, He will heal a demon-possessed boy. Through His limitless omniscience, He will prophecy His impending death. With sovereign certainty, He will instruct Peter how to fish for a coin to pay their temple tax. With each verse we read, Jesus demonstrates He is like nothing and no one who has ever walked the earth. Truly He is the most magnificent.

R   RECEIVING God's Word

Open in Prayer
Read Matthew 17

E   EXPERIENCING God's Word

Experience 1: Matthew 17:1–13

1. Read Matthew 17:1–2. Jesus took Peter, James, and John (his brother) up a high mountain and was transfigured before them. The word "transformed" is metamorphoó in the Greek. The Bible Lexicon defines it as "to change into another form." Describe how Jesus was changed before their eyes.

   a. Read Mark 9:3 and Luke 9:29. Mark and Luke also record details of the transfiguration of Jesus. What details do these writers add concerning Jesus' appearance?

2. Matthew 17:3 tells us that Elijah and Moses appeared to the disciples and were talking with Jesus. Elijah and Moses have significance in that Moses represents the Law that God gave to the Jews and Elijah represents the Prophets who spoke of things to come for Jesus and the future of the Jewish nation. Read Matthew 5:17. When Jesus came what was His purpose concerning the Jewish law and prophets?

3. Read Matthew 17:4. Peter makes a suggestion to Jesus about lodging on the mountain. Read Malachi 4:5–6. Think about prophecy and the timing of Elijah showing up on the mountain. Why would his appearance signal something more permanent in Peter's mind?

4. Read Matthew 17:5. Describe what is happening in this verse.

Delighting in the King of Kings

    a. In Matthew 17:5 God announced that Jesus is His beloved Son in Whom He is well pleased. These words were also spoken by God over Jesus in Matthew 3:17 when Jesus was baptized. These words authenticated Jesus' identity as the Son of God from the Father as Jesus began His earthly ministry. In Matthew 17:5 God is speaking the same words but now Elijah, Moses, and three disciples are present. Keeping in mind the future kingdom of heaven is still to come, why would God announce that Jesus is His Son again?

5. Read Matthew 17:6–8. When the disciples heard the voice come out of the cloud, what was their reaction, and how did Jesus reassure them?

6. Jesus gives the disciples a command in verse 9. Considering what you learned in question 3 of this lesson, why would it be very important for the disciples to obey Jesus' request? What might happen if they didn't obey?

    a. When did Jesus give them permission to share the event they just witnessed? Why is this timing important?

7. Read Matthew 17:10–13. The disciples appear to be unable to resolve in their minds the appearance of Elijah. They ask Jesus again to clarify why the scribes teach that Elijah has to come first. How does Jesus explain it to them? How does He factor in Elijah the Old Testament prophet, John the Baptist the New Testament prophet (Luke 1:16–17), and the Elijah of the future (Revelation 11:3–6) that is yet come?

Experience 2: Matthew 17:14–27

1. Read Matthew 17:14–16. Luke 9:37 states, "The next day when they came down from the mountain a large crowd met them." From this we will assume that these events followed the transfiguration. A man comes out of the crowd and kneels before Jesus sharing his struggle. Describe his situation.

2. Mark 9:19–29 details this same story but gives specific details about the father's faith. Read the verses in Mark. What do you learn about this man's faith in Jesus?

3. In Matthew 17:17 Jesus speaks to the disciples in response to what the man had to say in verses 14–16. What did Jesus call the disciples?

    a. Given all that has transpired in this chapter so far, why does Jesus seem so frustrated?

4. Read Matthew 17:18–21. Jesus immediately heals the child. The disciples watch Jesus do what they couldn't do, even though Jesus had given them healing power. They ask Jesus why they weren't able to cast out the demon. Jesus gives three reasons they lacked His power. What are they?

  a. Keep in mind as Peter, James, and John were on the mountain with Jesus, the other disciples were not. Scripture does not tell us what those disciples were doing while Jesus was gone. We also don't know how long Jesus and the three disciples were on the mountain. Based on verses 18–21, what do we know the others weren't doing that affected their ability to drive out the demon?

5. Read Matthew 17:22–23. What does Jesus tell His disciples, and what is their response?

6. Read Matthew 17:24–26. All Jewish men were required to give a half shekel as payment for the temple tax. The temple tax collector asks Peter about Jesus' payment. What do you observe about Jesus through His response to Peter?

  a. In verses 25–26 Jesus asks Peter a question about the temple tax. What point is Jesus making regarding His identity and responsibility?

7. Read Matthew 17:27. In Matthew 10:9 Jesus sent out His disciples without any money. Money was needed in this moment to pay the temple tax. Jesus gave a very creative solution to the problem and even incorporated Peter's former profession to solve it. What was it?

8. Write a short description of Jesus as the King of Kings from what you learned in this chapter.

 ### ACTING on God's Word

In this chapter we have been virtual witnesses to the greatness of Jesus and have studied some of His magnificent ways. He took on human flesh to clothe His deity and yet, despite being fully human, He also displayed His magnificence as being fully God. As we saw in this chapter, His ways have no boundaries. We have been given the extraordinary opportunity of knowing Him as our Lord and Savior, and all it takes is faith the size of a mustard seed to believe in Him. Worship should be our response to Jesus, for who He is and for all He has done for us. How can we, sinners, not praise Him? Yet I (Brenda) wonder how many hours a week we actually spend giving back our worship and thanksgiving to God. Considering all Jesus has done for us, I believe the least we can do is to return to Him our worship and praise.

1. Psalm 145 is a praise song written by King David to God. Read the Psalm and circle, highlight, or comment next to the text that most clearly expresses your worship back to the Lord.

   Psalm 145 New King James Version (NKJV)
   A Song of God's Majesty and Love
   A Praise of David

   I will extol You, my God, O King;
   And I will bless Your name forever and ever.
   2 Every day I will bless You,
   And I will praise Your name forever and ever.
   3 Great is the Lord, and greatly to be praised;
   And His greatness is unsearchable.
   4 One generation shall praise Your works to another,
   And shall declare Your mighty acts.
   5 I will meditate on the glorious splendor of Your majesty,
   And on Your wondrous works.
   6 Men shall speak of the might of Your awesome acts,
   And I will declare Your greatness.
   7 They shall utter the memory of Your great goodness,
   And shall sing of Your righteousness.
   8 The Lord is gracious and full of compassion,
   Slow to anger and great in mercy.
   9 The Lord is good to all,
   And His tender mercies are over all His works.
   10 All Your works shall praise You, O Lord,
   And Your saints shall bless You.
   11 They shall speak of the glory of Your kingdom,
   And talk of Your power,
   12 To make known to the sons of men His mighty acts,
   And the glorious majesty of His kingdom.

13 Your kingdom is an everlasting kingdom,
And Your dominion endures throughout all generations.
14 The LORD upholds all who fall,
And raises up all who are bowed down.
15 The eyes of all look expectantly to You,
And You give them their food in due season.
16 You open Your hand
And satisfy the desire of every living thing.
17 The LORD is righteous in all His ways,
Gracious in all His works.
18 The LORD is near to all who call upon Him,
To all who call upon Him in truth.
19 He will fulfill the desire of those who fear Him;
He also will hear their cry and save them.
20 The LORD preserves all who love Him,
But all the wicked He will destroy.
21 My mouth shall speak the praise of the LORD,
And all flesh shall bless His holy name
Forever and ever.

2. Write one phrase from the Psalm that you liked the most in a personal tribute to God for who He is and all that He has done.

 **D** **DELIGHTING** in God's Word

From Matthew 17, how has the Lord prompted you to pray?

Write a verse from the chapter that God has spoken to your heart.

Close in Prayer

"The one thing I ask of the Lord - the thing I seek most - is to live in the house of the Lord all the days of my life, delighting in the Lord's perfections and meditating in his temple." Psalm 27:4

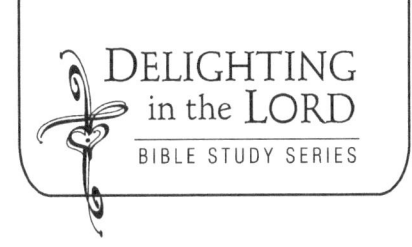

WEEK 9
THE KING'S LESSONS ON HUMILITY
Matthew 18

We live in a world that measures success and greatness by getting ahead, climbing the corporate ladder, wealth, and having many possessions. People love to display these achievements for all to see. Our society is marked by self-promotion, self-love, and looking out for Number 1—ourselves. When it comes to relationships, pride is often center stage. Relationships can be marked by who we know and how those we know can help us advance. The world's "climb to the top" attitude often steps on and over other people along the way. Well-known Bible commentator Warren Wiersbe said this—"By nature, all of us are rebels who want to be celebrities instead of servants. It takes a great deal of teaching for us to learn the lessons of humility." Is this the attitude and world you've bought into?

This is not what Jesus desires for the child of God. Pride is not a mark of His Kingdom citizens. Jesus will teach us in Matthew 18 many lessons on humility that permeate all aspects of our lives. He desires His children to live humbly. He demands we be humble before Him and with other people, especially when we are offended. There is no place for pride before Jesus. Where pride replaces humility, spiritual surgery is necessary. We will learn in this chapter that the truly humble person does not cause someone else to sin. When we sin, we should examine ourselves before God. "I'm sorry" and "please forgive me" should readily be on our lips. The humble person pursues and builds up other people, not for the sake of themselves but for the other's benefit. The humble person seeks to serve, not to be served. As we live humbly, others will see Jesus through us, the body of Christ will be built up, and we will live in restored relationships with one another. Can you imagine what our world would look like if more people lived with humility? It starts with me. It starts with you. After we finish this chapter, may humility no longer be a word we associate with weakness, but one we associate with greatness!

R RECEIVING God's Word

Open in Prayer
Read Matthew 18

E EXPERIENCING God's Word

Experience 1: Matthew 18:1–14

1. Read Matthew 18:1. As the disciples were pondering the coming kingdom of heaven, they came to Jesus and asked Him a question. Based on their question, what was their kingdom concern?

2. Read Matthew 18:2–4. Jesus could have used Himself as the object lesson for greatness, but He used a child instead. Why a child?

    a. In verse 3 Jesus uses the word "converted" as a requirement to enter the kingdom of heaven. *Converted* in the Greek is the word *strepho* which means "to turn." What was Jesus saying to the disciples by using the word *converted*?

    b. According to verse 4, how is greatness in God's kingdom measured? How does Luke 14:11 confirm this?

3. In Matthew 18:5 Jesus tells His disciples that when they receive a little child in His name it is like they are receiving Him. What does it mean to "receive" a little child in Jesus' name? How does this equate to receiving Jesus?

4. Jesus gives a stern warning in Matthew 18:6–7. What is that warning?

    a. In the warning Jesus gives in verse 6, He specifies those little ones "who believe in Me." What point is Jesus making?

b. How would someone cause a child to sin or lead a child into sin? Give examples.

c. Jesus references a millstone in verse 6. A millstone is a large stone used to grind grain. They often weighed well over 100lbs. What does this indicate about God's heart and the severity of the punishment for this offense?

5. Read Matthew 18:7. This verse starts with the word "Woe" which depicts the gravity of the warning. What is Jesus saying to the offender? Where will this leave those who have served in His church, yet misused one of those little ones?

6. Read Matthew 18:8–9 and answer the following questions:

a. What three body parts does Jesus address? Why?

b. Jesus is not talking in literal terms. Explain Jesus' warning concerning offenses. What is our responsibility?

c. Jesus contrasts current life with eternal life in regard to sin. What is Jesus saying?

7. What command is given in Matthew 18:10? Keep in mind that the word *despise* in the Greek means to "think down upon or against."

   a. Read Hebrews 1:14. How does this verse help you understand the role of the angels in Matthew 18:10?

8. Write verse 11 below. What did Jesus mean by using the word *lost*? What does this tell you about His heart?

9. Read Matthew 18:12–14.

   a. How does this parable illustrate the value Jesus places on individuals?

   b. What does this parable say regarding our care over the Christian community?

   c. What does this parable say regarding our care and love for sinners?

10. Read 1 Timothy 2:4. What is the heart of Jesus for every person?

Experience 2: Matthew 18:15–20

1. Read Matthew 18:15–20. What is Jesus teaching His disciples in these verses?

2. As a believer, what is our responsibility according to James 5:19–20?

3. Matthew 18:15 tells us clearly what should be done first when someone offends or sins against us. What should we do?

   a. What does *hearing* mean in this verse regarding the offender? What does it not mean?

4. According to verse 16, what is the next step to be taken if the first one is unsuccessful? What is the benefit of having witnesses with you according to this verse?

5. Read Matthew 18:17. We can't control a person's response. Our job is to obey God's command regarding our responsibility. If the offender refuses to receive what is being shared, what is the final action we should take?

6. Read Matthew 18:18. Remember in Matthew 16:19 this same concept was introduced regarding the authority to bind and loosen. Binding refers to what is not permitted and loosing refers to what is permitted. Why is this concept being used again in the context of offenses and restoration?

7. In Matthew 18:19–20 agreement and unity are introduced as a vital piece to restoration. How is agreement and unity achieved?

Experience 3: Matthew 18:21–35

1. Read Matthew 18:21–22. Peter asks Jesus about forgiveness. Jewish tradition limited forgiveness to three times. If someone wronged a Jew and asked for forgiveness, they were given three opportunities to be forgiven. If asked for, forgiveness needed to be granted by the third request. How did Jesus turn this tradition upside down with His answer?

2. Read Matthew 18:23–27. Jesus teaches Peter by using a parable. Keep in mind that ten thousand talents was a huge debt. Commentators have put the modern-day value somewhere between $12 million and $1 billion. Summarize the truth that Jesus was making regarding forgiveness and responsibility.

    a. How did the servant who owed the debt approach his master in verse 26?

    b. How did the master respond in verse 27?

3. Read Matthew 18:28. What does the servant, who was just forgiven of his enormous debt, do to his debtor after he was forgiven? Keep in mind that a denarius was a Roman silver coin worth about 16 cents, according to commentators. Matthew 20:2 tells us that a denarius was a typical day's wage for a laborer.

4. In Matthew 18:29 this debtor's response to the master's demand for payment is the same as seen in verse 26. How does the master, who had been forgiven of his debt, respond to the debtor in verse 30? What adjectives would you use to describe this master?

5. Read Matthew 18:31. Fellow servants witness all that happens between the master and debtor. How were they affected by what they witnessed in verse 31?

6. Read Matthew 18:32–34. The master calls the unforgiving servant "wicked" due to his lack of forgiveness. What qualities should have been demonstrated to the debtor?

   a. What was the unforgiving servant's consequence in verse 34?

7. What warning is given in verse 35 to all of us regarding God's heart toward unforgiveness?

8. Write a short description of Jesus as the King of Kings from what you learned in this chapter.

 **ACTING on God's Word**

1. <u>Humility as a Servant of God</u>

    In Matthew 18 Jesus used a child as an example of humility and greatness. Humility needs to be readily welcomed into our hearts. When we welcome humility, we are welcoming Christ into all parts of our life. It is a character quality not often esteemed in our culture but precious to God. On the contrary, pride is within our fallen human nature and often what is seen in people, especially where a degree of greatness is concerned.

a. 2 Chronicles 7:14 says, "if My people who are called by My name will humble themselves and pray and seek My face, and turn from their wicked ways, then I will hear from heaven, and will forgive their sin and heal their land." How does this verse stress the importance of humility in the life of the believer? How do you humble yourself before God?

b. Similar to the disciples, where does your thinking need to be "turned around" regarding greatness and humility?

2. Humility Regarding Sin

Jesus gives believers a warning about causing someone to sin, especially a child. When offenses occur, as they will, Jesus is clear that we must humbly take responsibility and address that sin. In Matthew 18:8–9 Jesus gave a radical example for addressing sin. It's that serious.

a. 1 John 1:8–9 says, "If we say that we have no sin, we deceive ourselves, and the truth is not in us. If we confess our sins, He is faithful and just to forgive us our sins and to cleanse us from all unrighteousness." How does humility operate where sin is present?

b. How does pride operate where sin is present?

c. Is there a sin in your life that needs to be humbly addressed before God right now? If so, spend time in prayer addressing it.

3. <u>Humility with Other People</u>

   a. You learned in Matthew 18:10 not to look down upon or against another believer. Practically speaking, how do people do this to others?

b. Is there someone in your life that you do this to? Explain. How would God have you help raise this person up instead of putting them down?

4. <u>Humility When Offended</u>

Matthew 18:15–35 addresses offenses and forgiveness. Jesus gave us clear instructions on how to deal with someone who sins against us. Jesus also taught on forgiveness when offenses happen. Jesus doesn't ask us to do something He hasn't done. He knows forgiveness well. He came to redeem the lost. He paid our sin penalty by wiping away our debt before God and restoring us to a right relationship with Him. He paid the debt with His very life, suffering beyond what we can even comprehend. With all humility, He went to the cross for you and me. He forgives us of our sins and gives us abundant life in this world and eternal life with Him in heaven. Take a minute and meditate on what Jesus did for you in your offense and debt.

a. Think of the last time someone offended you. How did you respond?

b. Based on what you learned today, how is humility a necessary ingredient in how we handle offenses? What can you apply from what you learned to a current offense?

c. Forgiveness is a choice. We can either forgive or keep adding to the offense sheet of an individual. Do you forgive easily? If not, what do you do; hold a grudge, let resentment build, talk about that person to others, give them the silent treatment/avoid them, think unkind thoughts toward them? Ephesians 4:32 says, "And be kind to one another, tender-hearted, forgiving one another, even as God in Christ forgave you." With humility, how can you apply this level of forgiveness to someone in your life whom you have not forgiven?

 **DELIGHTING** in God's Word

From Matthew 18, how has the Lord prompted you to pray?

Write a verse from the chapter that God has spoken to your heart.

Close in Prayer

"The one thing I ask of the Lord - the thing I seek most - is to live in the house of the Lord all the days of my life, delighting in the Lord's perfections and meditating in his temple." Psalm 27:4

WEEK 10
THE KING GOES TO THE HEART
Matthew 19

C.H. Spurgeon is quoted as saying, "The same sun which melts wax hardens clay. And the same Gospel which melts some persons to repentance hardens others in their sins." The sun, as described by Spurgeon, remains constant. It is steady, bright, and warm. However, it is the wax and clay which respond differently to the sun; one melts and the other hardens. It is not the sun but the response of the material to the sun that determines the effect. Spurgeon likens the sun to Christ in this analogy. The wax and the clay are like humanity when they hear the Gospel. Some will be pliable and receive Christ while others will become hardened and reject Him. The heart condition of the person determines the level of pliability to receive Christ and the willingness to be molded into His image.

There are four types of hearts described in Matthew 19. The Pharisees come to Jesus to test Him and to see how He will answer their questions on the topic of divorce. Jesus will describe their hearts as hardened, much like the clay Spurgeon described. A rich, young man will seek out Jesus to try and figure out how to obtain eternal life; however, his heart is divided between his riches and Christ. The disciples will raise a set of questions as well for Jesus. He will address their hearts' desires for equity and fairness in the life to come. But there is one group with soft and impressionable hearts who will be brought to Jesus; the children. The disciples will try to turn them away; however, Jesus will encourage them to come to Him because the kingdom of heaven is made up of people like them.

How do we approach Jesus? Do we come to Him with a soft and moldable heart or a hard and unyielding heart? When we seek Him, do we come like a doubtful Pharisee or a welcoming child? Matthew recorded the stories in Matthew 19 so that his readers could see man's heart condition and Jesus' steady response of love and truth. May we all grow more and more pliable and be conformed into His image as He steadily shines upon us.

RECEIVING God's Word

Open in Prayer
Read Matthew 19

EXPERIENCING God's Word

Experience 1: Matthew 19:1–15

1. Read Matthew 19:1–3. Picture what Jesus is doing as the Pharisees arrive to test Him. Describe the contrast between Jesus' mission and their mission.

    a. What is the question the Pharisees ask Jesus?

    b. Based on what we know about John the Baptist's imprisonment, why would Jesus' answer need to be worded carefully? (Matthew 14:3–4)

Delighting in the King of Kings

2. Jesus avoids getting into controversy with the Pharisees over divorce by explaining why people should stay married. Read Matthew 19:4–6 and answer the following questions:

   a. How many wives did God give Adam when He created him in the beginning? (Genesis 1:27, 5:2)

   b. What does the wording "one flesh" suggest about the permanency of the relationship? Can one flesh be separated easily?

   c. How do Jesus' words "let no man separate" conclude His answer well?

3. The Pharisees do not seem satisfied with the answer Jesus gives them, and therefore ask another question regarding marriage. Read Matthew 19:7–9 and answer the following questions:

   a. What do the Pharisees want to know about Moses' command regarding divorce? (Deuteronomy 24:1–4)

    b. Notice the difference between the word "command" the Pharisees used in verse 7 and the word "permit" used by Jesus in verse 8. How is Jesus correcting them before answering their question?

    c. How does Jesus explain the reason why Moses permitted divorce? (verse 8)

    d. Jesus gives an answer in verse 9. How is His answer a clarification to the Law?

4. The disciples have a follow-up statement for Jesus about marriage. Read Matthew 19:10–12. What statement did they make to Jesus in verse 10?

    a. Based on Jesus' answer in verse 11, who should remain single?

b. In verse 12 Jesus explains how a person becomes a eunuch. A eunuch is a man who has been castrated. According to Jesus in verse 12, why would Jesus suggest he stay single?

5. Jesus has just finished speaking about marriage. It was God's plan from the beginning for a married couple, one man and one woman, to come together as one flesh so the fruit of that union can bring the blessing of a child. Read Matthew 19:13–15. Who has been brought to Jesus in verse 13, and what are the parents looking for Jesus to do?

   a. The disciples did not want the children to come to Jesus. Describe Jesus' response to the disciples.

Experience 2: Matthew 19:16–30

1. Read Matthew 19:16–17 and Psalm 53:1–3. What do you learn about man's goodness from these verses?

    a. How does the man describe Jesus? What point is Jesus trying to make to this young man about His identity based on man's goodness?

    b. What question does the young man ask Jesus, and what is Jesus' answer to him?

2. Read Matthew 19:18–20 and Exodus 20:12–17. What commands does Jesus tell the man to follow in accordance with the Law? How does the young man respond?

3. Read Matthew 19:21–22. Based on these verses, what does Jesus suggest he do before he follows Him?

    a. What word is used in verse 22 to describe the man's emotion when he left? Based on the man's reaction, what hinders him from following Jesus?

4. After the exchange with the young man, Jesus turns to teach His disciples. Read Matthew 19:23–24. What does Jesus say about how wealth can inhibit a person from entering the kingdom of heaven?

    a. How does Jesus use a camel and a needle to explain the difficulty of loving both money and God equally?

5. Read Matthew 19:25–26. What reaction do the disciples have regarding the teaching Jesus just gave them? Jesus encourages them by telling them how they can be saved. What is His answer?

6. Read Matthew 19:27–30 and answer the following questions:

   a. Peter asks Jesus a question in verse 27. What is the nature of his question?

   b. Jesus replies to Peter in verses 28–29. There are rewards described by Jesus in these verses. In your own words, describe the reward and who it will be given to.

   c. Jesus gives a surprising statement in verse 30 regarding those who humbly and perhaps invisibly serve Him. What is it? What does this mean?

> "You remember the old Romish legend, which contains a great truth. There was a brother who preached very mightily, and who had won many souls to Christ, and it was revealed to him one night, in a dream, that in heaven he would have no reward for all that he had done. He asked to whom the reward would go; and an angel told him that it would go to an old man who used to sit on the pulpit stairs and pray for him. Well, it may be so, though it is more likely that both would share their Master's praise. We shall not be rewarded, however, simply according to our apparent success." (David Guzik quoting Spurgeon, www.blueletterbible.org)

7. Write a short description of Jesus as the King of Kings from what you learned in this chapter.

ACTING on God's Word

In the opening paragraph of the lesson, I (Brenda) gave you a quote by Spurgeon that likened mankind's heart to either wax or clay in the way it responds to Christ. The stories Matthew included in Matthew 19 demonstrate what it looked like to have a hardened heart, a greedy heart, and a desire for equity within the heart. Only the children had hearts that were soft and pliable toward Jesus. I think most of us desire to have a soft heart toward the Lord, but there is typically something standing in the way between us and Jesus. Let's take a closer look at what can cause a heart to harden and what can bring about a softened heart.

A Hard Heart

1. Hebrews 3:15 says, "Today, if you will hear His voice, do not harden your hearts." How does this verse put some of the responsibility for our heart's posture on us? Give examples of what a hard heart might look like toward God.

2. Has there been a time when you have chosen to harden your heart against God regarding something the Holy Spirit has prompted you to change, and yet you refused? Describe this situation and what resulted.

3. James 4:6 tells us that "God resists the proud but gives grace to the humble." How does pride factor into a hard heart? How have you personally seen this?

A Divided Heart

4. Matthew 6:24 says, "No one can serve two masters; for he will hate the one and love the other, or else he will be loyal to the one and despise the other. You cannot serve God and money." In Matthew 19:22 the rich young ruler, who came to Jesus seeking eternal life, left sorrowful because of his possessions. He

was unwilling to choose Jesus above his wealth. Has wealth or possessions ever hindered you in your walk with Jesus? How does wealth have the power to cause our hearts to be divided?

    a. Give practical examples of how wealth and possessions can be put in their rightful place before God.

An Equitable Heart

5. In Matthew 19:27 the disciples tell Jesus of their sacrifices for Him and ask Him what they will receive for all they've done. Their response seems to say,

"What about me?" Have you ever found yourself reminding God of things you've done for Him, hoping He'll show you favor for your sacrifices? What is wrong with this thinking?

A Soft Heart

6. In Matthew 19 Jesus used children as an example of those with soft hearts who receive the kingdom of heaven. Describe how a child often trusts and believes those in authority over them. Have you ever witnessed a child demonstrate a soft heart in a situation? Describe this situation. How is this an example for you to follow?

7. List the characteristics of a soft heart. Is there an area you struggle with more than another? If so, explain.

8. Close out your study time with prayer asking God to soften your heart in any area that is not fully surrendered to Him. You may write the prayer below or say it silently.

D DELIGHTING in God's Word

From Matthew 19, how has the Lord prompted you to pray?

Write a verse from the chapter that God has spoken to your heart.

Close in Prayer

"The one thing I ask of the Lord - the thing I seek most - is to live in the house of the Lord all the days of my life, delighting in the Lord's perfections and meditating in his temple." Psalm 27:4

WEEK 11
SERVANT OF THE KING
Matthew 20

The room was full of women standing and applauding as I (Brenda) walked away from the podium. It was only the third time I had taught God's Word publicly, but the first time I had such an overwhelming response to what I had shared. I was grateful God had taken the little I brought and multiplied it to encourage the women in attendance. An odd sense of pride began to well up alongside my gratitude. As I tried to push the prideful thoughts aside, I felt the Holy Spirit quickly rebuke me saying, "Be careful how you respond to the praise you receive, or it will be your only reward." I'm not sure what surprised me more, the applause from the ladies or the Holy Spirit's rebuke!

Although I have been teaching God's Word for over ten years, the lesson I learned was etched upon my heart. Shortly after that day, I decided to write at the top of each message three simple words in bold red letters which reads "Audience of One." As a servant of Christ, I do not work for the applause of those I serve but rather to please God. My responsibility is to be faithful to do the work He calls me to do and to be careful to give the praise to Him alone. I do not work expecting anything in return. I believe that offering my life back to the Lord is my reasonable act of service unto Him (Romans 12:1). If God chooses to bless me, I gladly receive it, but if He does not, I accept that as well. It is my goal to serve freely and without expectation, knowing full well that all I really deserve is an eternity separated from God. Therefore, even if I am only given my salvation, I have already gotten far more than I deserve. I'm thankful I learned this concept early on in ministry.

Perhaps Jesus wanted to be sure His disciples approached their ministry for Him with a similar attitude. If you recall, at the end of Matthew 19 Peter raised a question regarding what he and the other disciples would receive because they had left everything behind to follow Him. Jesus told them they would be judges over Israel, sit on thrones, and in addition to being given a hundredfold, they would receive eternal life. My guess is that they were pretty enthusiastic over this news but maybe a bit too enthusiastic.

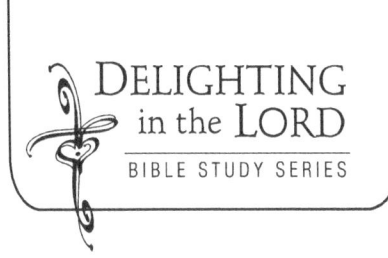

Chapter 20 is a continuation of the conversation Jesus had with His disciples in chapter 19. The chapter begins with Jesus teaching the disciples in the form of a parable about rewards given to servants. It reiterates the point from Matthew 19 that "the first will be last and the last first." That's what rewards and service look like in God's kingdom. Jesus continues to tell them how He would die, addresses a bold request from the mother of James and John, and then closes out the chapter with a miraculous healing of two blind men. We are certainly not short on interesting content in this chapter.

As you begin your study time in prayer, ask the Lord to show you any expectations of reward you may feel you deserve for the service you have done in His name. May we each joyfully, freely, and without expectation serve our Savior from now until He calls us to be with Him in His kingdom, knowing that our salvation is more than enough of a generous gift.

RECEIVING God's Word

Open in Prayer
Read Matthew 20

EXPERIENCING God's Word

Experience 1: Matthew 20:1–16

As we move into chapter 20, Jesus is now going to use a parable to answer Peter's question with an illustration. Remember what you learned in chapter 13 about a parable. It takes a spiritual lesson and places it beside an earthly example in order to illustrate one main point. It is how Jesus often taught the multitudes and disciples in an effort to drive a point to their hearts in a simple way. Keep that in mind as you answer these questions.

1. Read Matthew 20:1–16. This parable is used to explain the kingdom of heaven. Who do you think is the landowner and who are the laborers? What do the vineyard and the payment represent? Fill in the chart with what you think each represents.

Landowner	
Laborers	
Vineyard	
Denarius	

A denarius would have equaled a day's wage. Notice it was a 12-hour work day that began around 6:00 A.M. The third hour would have been about 9:00 A.M., the sixth hour about 12 noon, and the eleventh hour was about 5:00 P.M. (Ironside).

2. This parable in Matthew 20:1–16 is not an illustration about earning salvation through works. Read 2 Timothy 1:8–9 and Ephesians 2:8–9 and explain why. How does one receive salvation?

3. Read Matthew 20:2. What agreement is made between the landowner and the first set of laborers?

4. What word do you see repeated three times in verses 2–6? (NKJV). Why is this word significant within the context of this parable?

5. Read Matthew 20:7. How is the agreement with the later laborers different from the first set of laborers? What does this agreement demonstrate about the relationship between the landowner and the workers?

6. Read Matthew 20:8–16 and answer the following questions:

   a. The landowner has the steward pay the laborers at the end of the day. In what order does he pay the workers? (vs. 8)

   b. What did all the laborers receive as their wage? (vs. 9–10)

   c. Using verses 10–12, describe the attitude of the laborers who were hired at the start of day upon receiving their wages according to:

   Expectations—

   Comparisons—

   Inequality—

   Passing judgment—

d. The landowner addresses the complaints of the early laborers by reminding them of their agreement at the time of their hire. How does he explain his actions according to verses 14–15, and why was their thinking flawed?

7. What phrase do you see in verse 16 repeated from chapter 19? How do these words take on new meaning following the teaching of this parable? Rewrite this phrase using your own words.

8. Going back to Peter's question in Matthew 19:27, what was Peter looking for, and how did Jesus use this parable to answer Peter's question? What was the main point of this parable, and how is this a point for all of us to understand regarding our service to the Lord?

9. With the understanding that God is likened unto the landowner in this parable, check all the things you learned about God's character from verses 1–16.

   ___God is fair
   ___God requires us to work for our salvation
   ___God cares more about length of service than faithfulness in serving
   ___God is generous
   ___God does not give good gifts
   ___God is gracious
   ___God is true to His Word
   ___God is a slave driver when it comes to work and service
   ___God sees our hearts
   ___God loves to give gifts and rewards to his faithful servants

10. Read 1 Corinthians 3:5–8. Describe what these verses say about the work-and-reward relationship from God's perspective.

Experience 2: Matthew 20:17–28

1. Read Matthew 20:17–19. Keep in mind this is Jesus' final entrance into Jerusalem before the events He details will take place. In these verses Jesus speaks prophetically once again as to what will happen to Him. Similar words were spoken previously in Matthew 16:21 and Matthew 17:22–23, but this was the first time He spoke of His crucifixion. List the order of events which are to come.

    a. Considering His recent teaching to the disciples about servanthood in His kingdom, why would Jesus prophesy about His suffering, death, and resurrection?

2. Read Matthew 20:20–21. Salome is believed to be the mother of James and John, who were also known as Zebedee's sons. She and her sons came to Jesus and made a request. What was it?

    a. Read Mark 10:35–37. What additional information did you learn from this account that was not included in Matthew's account of the same events?

3. Read Matthew 20:22. Jesus spoke into the ignorance of the request made to Him. How did He answer them, and what does this imply about their understanding or lack thereof?

4. James and John boldly answer Jesus in verse 22 by speaking of their ability, even though they didn't understand what Jesus meant. Read Matthew 20:23. Jesus affirms that they will experience some of what He would go through in the days to come.

   a. Read Acts 12:1–2. What will happen to James?

   b. Read Acts 4:1–3 and Revelation 1:9. John wrote first, second and third John as well as Revelation. The 2nd century North African theologian, Tertullian, reports that John was plunged in hot oil by the Romans and survived. What do you learn from these verses in Acts and Revelation about John's suffering?

> Salome learned her lesson. When Jesus was crucified, she was standing near the cross (John 19:25, "His mother's sister") and sharing in His sorrow and pain. She did not see two thrones on either side of her Lord—she saw two thieves on crosses. And she heard Jesus give her son John to His mother, Mary. Salome's selfishness was rebuked, and she meekly accepted it. (Warren Wiersbe, *Be Loyal*, pg. 186)

5. According to verses 22–23, who grants position and honor in the kingdom of God?

6. Matthew 20:24 says that upon hearing this conversation, the disciples were displeased with James and John. In your opinion, why might they have been upset?

7. Read Matthew 20:25–28. In these verses there is a beautiful picture of Jesus' purpose and attributes portrayed. What are they?

8. The Jews in Jesus' day would have been accustomed to the Gentile, Roman rulership. In verses 26–28, how did Jesus describe power and status in His kingdom compared to the way the disciples were ruled under Roman leadership?

   a. Look back at Matthew 20:17–19 and compare it with Matthew 20:27–28. Using these two sets of scriptures, how are we to live our lives based on the example Jesus gave us?

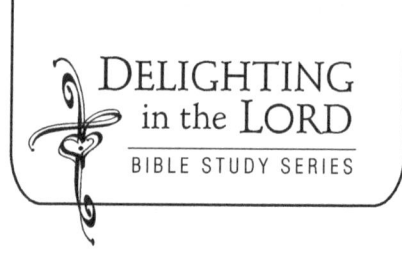

9. Look up the following verses and note how God measures greatness.

   a. Matthew 18:4

   b. Matthew 23:11

   c. Philippians 2:5–9

Experience 3: Matthew 20:29–34

1. Read the account of the blind men in Matthew 20:29–34. Write down anything from these verses that stands out to you.

   a. The same account about the blind men is recorded in Mark 10:46–52 and Luke 18:35–43. Read these verses and note any additional details you learn.

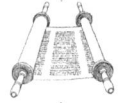

2. Notice the title the blind men used for Jesus in Matthew 20:30. Read 2 Samuel 7:12–16 about the prophecy that Nathan the prophet spoke to King David. Why is this title significant?

> Had [the two blind men as recorded in Matthew] cried to Him as Jesus of Nazareth or simply as "Lord" their witness would have not fitted into the scene at all. But as the Son of David and Heir to the throne of David, He was to be presented to Jerusalem, and ere this takes place He has the witness of two witnesses that He is the Son of David. [This is the last recorded miracle of Jesus before He enters Jerusalem for the last time.] According to the law the testimony of two witnesses was necessary. (*The Gospel of Matthew: An Exposition* by Arno C. Gaebelein, pg. 419)

3. These blind men knew in their hearts something about Jesus that the multitudes following Him did not. How does the response of the multitudes in verse 31 convey this?

4. Read Matthew 20:32–34. How did Jesus heal these men?

5. Write a short description of Jesus as the King of Kings from what you learned in this chapter.

 **ACTING on God's Word**

I'm (Stacy) not telling you something you don't know. We live in a very "me-focused" culture. In so many areas like social media, relationships, and even our walk with God, things can quickly turn inward making everything in life be about us. To make matters worse, in the "me mentality" we can look for recognition, rewards, and even status so people have more of a reason to look at us.

The world tells us to look out for number one. We take pictures of ourselves, call them selfies, and post them to social media. If we are honest, they are our own self-run marketing campaign. Then, we look at everyone else's marketing campaign and tend to judge our lives against what we see in someone else's social media posts. The comparison trap is constantly before our eyes through the words and images we allow to consume our time. It's easy to feel left out, less than, and not enough.

In Matthew 20 Jesus' disciples and a mother wrestle with the "me mentality." With great patience and love, Jesus turned their thinking upside down because His kingdom does not operate according to the world's view.

1. Based on what you learned in Matthew 20, how is the kingdom of heaven's work, reward, and status different from the world's system?

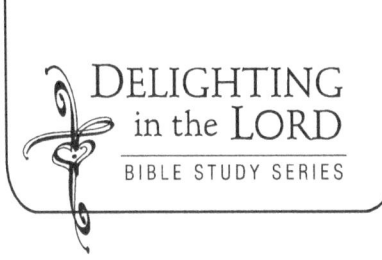

a. Has the world's work-and-reward system defined your perspective in any way? Below is a list of possible ways it might. Check off all that apply to you.

___ If I work hard, I will be rewarded more than someone who doesn't work hard.

___ Compensation motivates my work and time.

___ I deserve to be recognized for my work. When I'm not, I get hurt and angry.

___ It's not fair when someone else gets rewarded for what I did.

___ I desire a position of prominence and/or title. It makes me feel valued.

___ I desire my work and effort to be noticed by others.

___ I expect people to do things for me more so than me doing for others.

___ I like to have ownership of the things I do. It's my work to do.

___ I am self-sufficient. I don't need the help of others and don't desire it.

___ I have become self-righteous, thinking I'm better than others because of all I do for the Lord.

___ other: _____

b. Look at the areas you checked. Based on what you learned today, how is this perspective flawed in God's kingdom? Rewrite any areas you checked to reflect God's perspective on status, work, and rewards.

  c. Now apply this perspective to any area of ministry. Have you found this perspective has carried over from everyday life to areas of service for God? Explain.

2. Below is a list of "me-mentality" perspectives we saw in Matthew 20. Have you struggled with any of these? If so, explain.

- "Woe is me" (Matthew 20:11–12)

- "Me first" (Matthew 20:21)

- "What about me" (Matthew 20:24)

- "Me too" (Matthew 20:29–34)

3. Explain in your own words what Jesus meant in Matthew 20:27–28: "And whoever desires to be first among you, let him be your slave—just as the Son of Man did not come to be served, but to serve, and to give His life a ransom for many."

4. Now, apply Matthew 20:27–28 to:

   a. Your relationships (wife, mother, friend, daughter, sister etc.):

   b. Your work inside the home and/or outside the home:

   c. Your ministry/areas of service:

 **DELIGHTING** in God's Word

From Matthew 20, how has the Lord prompted you to pray?

Write a verse from the chapter that God has spoken to your heart.

Close in Prayer

"The one thing I ask of the Lord - the thing I seek most - is to live in the house of the Lord all the days of my life, delighting in the Lord's perfections and meditating in his temple." Psalm 27:4

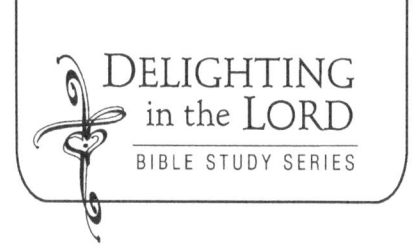

BIBLIOGRAPHY

Gaebelein, Arno C. *The Gospel of Matthew: An Exposition*. Loizeaux Brothers, 1977.

Guzik, David. "The Enduring Word Bible Commentary." *Enduring Word*, enduringword.com.

Ironside, H.A. *Matthew: Ironside Commentaries*. Loizeaux Brothers, 1994.

McGee, J. Vernon. *Thru the Bible Commentary, Volume 35: Matthew Chapters 14–28*. Thomas Nelson, 1991.

Radmacher, Earl D., et al. *The NKJV Study Bible*. New King James Version. 2nd ed., Thomas Nelson, 2007.

Walvoord, John F., and Roy B. Zuck. *Bible Knowledge Commentary*. David C. Cook, 1983.

Wiersbe, Warren W. *Be Loyal: Following the King of Kings*. David C. Cook, 2008.

www.blueletterbible.org

www.britannica.com/biography/Saint-John-the-Apostle

www.clipart-library.com/torah-cliparts.html

www.en.oxforddictionaries.com/definition/criticism

www.merriam-webster.com/dictionary/blasphemy

www.spurgeon.org